'Dr Arbouin expertly weaves the educatic
professionals into a wider nuanced analysis of
of the education system on the lives of black
work and an essential read for educato_

**Dr William Ackah, Programme Director, Community Development and
Globalisation, Birkbeck, University of London**

'Compelling and enlightening! This new book explores and chronicles the
challenges, experiences and the successful outcomes of black graduates. Dr
Arbouin's book complements the growing body of literature on resiliency,
personal stories and person-centred ethnographies. I highly recommend
this book for anyone interested in real solutions and creating genuine
opportunities for future generations of black students who dream of going
to University one day and graduating.'

**Dr Richard Majors, former Clinical Fellow, Harvard Medical School, and
Honorary Professor, University of Colorado, Colorado Springs**

'This is an original and much needed book charting the trajectories of
black graduates. The insights are telling and revealing. There is much to
learn here for educational policymakers in schools and higher education.
The implications for the future employment of black graduates are
immense. This is compelling reading for all involved in education.'

**Professor Cecile Wright, School of Sociology and Social Policy,
University of Nottingham**

# Black British Graduates

# Black British Graduates
## Untold stories

Amanda Arbouin

 is an imprint of

First published in 2018 by the UCL Institute of Education Press, 20 Bedford Way, London WC1H 0AL

www.ucl-ioe-press.com

©2018 Amanda Arbouin

British Library Cataloguing in Publication Data:
A catalogue record for this publication is available from the British Library

ISBNs
978-1-85856-8539 (paperback)
978-1-85856-8546 (PDF eBook)
978-1-85856-8553 (ePub eBook)
978-1-85856-8560 (Kindle eBook)

Every effort has been made to trace copyright holders and to obtain their permission for the use of copyright material. The publisher apologizes for any errors or omissions and would be grateful if notified of any corrections that should be incorporated in future reprints or editions of this book.

The opinions expressed in this publication are those of the author and do not necessarily reflect the views of the UCL Institute of Education.

Typeset by Quadrant Infotech (India) Pvt Ltd
Printed by CPI Group (UK) Ltd, Croydon, CR0 4YY
Cover image by Mary Alice Hinkley, © 2013 UCL Creative Media Services

# Contents

# List of tables

# About the author

*Dr Amanda Arbouin* is a Senior Lecturer in Education Studies at the Nottingham Institute of Education. She has taught in higher education, further education and industry for a number of years and has also undertaken project management, research and consultancy.

Her first book, *Black British Graduates: Untold stories*, examines the educational journeys and career outcomes of a group of British graduates of African-Caribbean parentage. Her research interests include:

- sociology of education encompassing the structuring effects of race/ethnicity, social class and gender
- social justice and the conditions that facilitate educational attainment and inclusion
- social science research methodology, including qualitative and quantitative approaches and techniques.

Dr Arbouin is pursuing opportunities for collaborative international research with a particular focus on black and minoritized students in the UK, the Caribbean and the USA.

Photo: David Baird

# Acknowledgements

I would like to express my gratitude to all of the research participants for their time and willingness to share their experiences and views, which made this research possible. I would also like to thank all the unnamed people who have offered me encouragement and guidance along the way. Finally, I would like to thank Kaya, Paul, Mom and Michelle, whose love and support have kept me going.

Inspiration for the book's subtitle, 'Untold stories', came from one of my favourite songs by the Jamaican reggae artist Buju Banton. Every time I hear his words 'What is to stop the youths from get out of control, Full up of education yet no own no payroll', I grieve for the many black graduates in the UK who, despite playing by the rules, find themselves struggling to reap the rewards in a society that continues to stack the odds against them. I dedicate this book to them and all those who seek to redress the balance by striving for social justice.

# Chapter 1

# An introduction

This book focuses on the careers and educational experiences of a group of black[1] British graduates of African-Caribbean parentage. In this chapter I explain the rationale for the research project, identifying gaps in the existing literature and what this book offers. I demarcate its scope, clarify the research aims and questions, outline my methodological approach and provide an overview of the other chapters.

The book is the first to document the life chances of black graduates in the UK, bringing the evidence of their experiences to print. It considers the value of education by exploring the career outcomes and educational journeys of these graduates in light of the existing literature on race, class and gender in compulsory education, post-compulsory education and careers. I also bring together these domains to consider the structural trajectory across them for black learners.

Using a life trajectory research approach, the research spans the entire educational experience and career outcomes of the group of black British graduates. The original research was completed in 2009, when most participants were in their thirties and forties and well into their professional careers. Their schooling spanned the 1970s and 1980s, and their university experiences were in the 1980s, 1990s and 2000s. The passage of time enhanced the research, presenting a long view of their experiences and adding a social history dynamic. Participants identified the factors they perceived as instrumental in helping or hindering their progress through education. Current statistics indicate that the inequalities participants identify are still central to black learners' experience in the education system today and point to the urgent need for policies to address this.

In contrast to most literature on race and education, this book focuses on the success of black learners. As the research participants are graduates they are educational achievers. However, statistically, black learners are more likely to leave school with below-average GCSE outcomes (Education Commission, 2004; DfE, 2015), showing that they are being failed en masse by the British education system. This has a negative impact on their individual career prospects and the wider socio-economic effect is that black communities are, to a great extent, marginalized and ghettoized. Despite being graduates, many of my research participants felt that they did not fulfil their potential in school. So an assessment of what they consider to be the contributory factors to their early underachievement in compulsory education and their later success in post-compulsory education opens up a new and particularly useful area.

The book also considers the marked gender differential among black learners. It is rare to find black male and female experiences of education explored in tandem. Instead, much of the literature on race in higher education addresses men's and women's experiences jointly, collapsing the analysis of the two cohorts into one. When the spotlight is on race and gender, black women's experiences tend to be the focus in post-compulsory education and black boys' experiences the focus in schools. There is a dearth of research relating to black males in the higher education context and I address this hiatus in the literature.

The main objective of the book is to present the viewpoints of the participants and so there is no in-depth discussion of the various amendments to education policy during the period. However, policy innovations inevitably inform the analyses within my book and I highlight the policy implications in the concluding chapter.

## Research aims
The research had two major aims:

- To gain insight into the educational experiences and career outcomes of black graduates who were born and educated entirely in the UK.
- To explore participants' perceptions of their graduate careers and of the education system from compulsory schooling in childhood through to graduation from UK higher education institutions.

Successive governments since the early 1990s have declared an educational agenda of widening participation and social inclusion that will lead to social mobility. The idea is that encouraging a broader cross-section of society to become involved in education will ultimately upskill the workforce and increase economic prosperity.

There is over-representation of black women in continuing education and under-representation of black men (Mirza, 1997; Reynolds, 2006; HESA, 2008). There are also significant differences in the performance of black boys and girls in school (EHRC, 2011). At the same time, media coverage pathologizes black communities by focusing on the underachievement of black learners in education, while paying little attention to the structures of oppression that create that situation. Channer (1995) suggests that:

> If [the] socio-economic factors and the aspirations of black families were as fully examined as negative stereotypes, the education and sociological literature might take account of the extent to which educational aspirations have been suppressed in black children ... destroyed and nullified.
>
> (Channer, 1995: 86)

In order to rectify this stifling scenario, we need to introduce positive measures to improve the career prospects and educational achievement of black learners. To achieve this, research that gives prominence to experiences of education from a black perspective is essential. hooks (1989) succinctly asserts the importance of black perspectives being presented in research about race:

> Even if perceived 'authorities' writing about a group to which they do not belong and/or over which they wield power, are progressive, caring and right-on in every way, as long as their authority is constituted either by the absence of the voices of the individuals whose experience they seek to address, or the dismissal of those voices as unimportant, the subject/object dichotomy is maintained and domination is reinforced ... When we write about experiences of a group to which we do not belong, we should think about the ethics of our action, considering whether or not our work will be used to reinforce and perpetuate domination.
>
> (hooks, 1989: 43)

## Methodological issues

A qualitative research approach underpinned the research methodology and this is ideal for a small-scale project that seeks depth of understanding as opposed to measurement and prediction (McKernan, 1991). The main data collection comprised a series of semi-structured interviews that followed a life history and narrative approach. This methodological approach complements black oral history traditions and women's 'ways of knowing' (Collins, 2000). It is also an appropriate way of giving voice to those who frequently go unheard (Asher, 2001). My use of direct quotes from the research participants foregrounds their powerful narratives.

## Design of the study

The overarching research questions were:

- How do black graduates experience the structures of race, class and gender in employment and educational settings?
- What resources do black graduates draw upon to navigate these domains and enable their successes?
- In what ways do black graduates consider it important to use their skills and experiences to challenge the inequalities of race, class and gender in British society?

Triangulation is 'often cited as one of the central ways of "validating" qualitative research evidence' (Ritchie and Lewis, 2003: 43) and this multi-method approach provides a way of cross-checking data to ensure that feedback and conclusions are not biased by the technique (Bell, 1993). Accordingly, I collected qualitative, quantitative and secondary data, which I compared and contrasted to ensure the veracity of my interpretations.

In relation to the primary data, I carried out a total of 50 hours of in-depth, semi-structured interviews, comprised of five hours with each of the ten participants. I supplemented this data by using questionnaires, interviewee diaries and my own research diary. The questionnaires provided some quantitative data while interviewee diaries gave a one-week snapshot into the participants' working lives. My position as a black, female academic enabled me to make first-hand observations about the impacts of race, class and gender within academic environments, which I recorded in my own research diary.

I obtained secondary data through an ongoing review of the literature on (a) minoritized[2] graduates' careers and (b) race, class and gender in education. I also reviewed institutional policy documents and reports relating to widening participation policies. As the participants' stories unfolded, constant reflection on the literature and emerging themes was essential.

## Sampling

I selected a purposive sample of ten black graduates of African-Caribbean parentage who had been educated entirely in the British education system. In order to reflect the experiences across both genders I chose five men and five women. All were in their thirties at the start of the research and this not only enabled me to explore the impact of their education on their careers, but also to build a picture of their progression through the whole education system. Summative participant biographies are in the Appendix.

I chose not to use a white British control group since I could draw comparisons from the considerable literature that centres on white experiences. I was mindful that all white studies do not require a black control group to validate them (Solórzano, 1998) and I wanted to avoid the risk in social research of pathologizing black experiences and perspectives by measuring them against a white 'norm' (Karenga, 1993). Critical race theory suggests that black people know from their experiences things that white people may not know or understand, because of their different experience of race (Solórzano, 1998). I therefore resolved to undertake the research purely from a black perspective, acknowledging that the participants were 'knowing subjects' and experts on their own lives, who would be able to offer insights into issues central to their viewpoint.

As a member of the black community and a graduate, I was able to use my own contacts as the starting point for identifying a snowball sample. Once I had made initial contacts within the desired population, I obtained other contacts from them and yet further contacts from those. Thus, the snowball effect occurred and continued until I had the desired number of participants for the sample population.

## Data collection and analysis

A grounded theory approach (Glaser and Strauss, 1967) ensured that the primary data generated themes that became the main focus of the research analysis. The process of analysis was cyclical: it entailed identifying themes and then refining and revisiting them.

Interviewees completed questionnaires before the first series of interviews and I used SPSS quantitative analysis software to identify the themes that emerged from the responses. These shaped the questions in the interview schedules and stimulated further discussion during the interviews.

Three semi-structured interviews were carried out with each participant at one-year intervals. Extending the primary research over two years gave an ongoing insight into their lives. The interview schedules contained a handful of open-ended questions for discussion with the participants. The first interview focused on race and higher education, the second on identity, and the third on the relationship between political awareness and education. Open-ended questions allowed the respondents to talk in a natural way about the topic and provided opportunities for the interviewees to bring in details they felt were pertinent to the topic. NVivo qualitative analysis software enabled me to organize and code data into first broad, and then narrower, categories and thereby explore the interconnection of the emergent themes and sub-themes.

In the past objectivity was held up as the ideal for good research and validity, but it is now widely accepted that 'objectivity is in fact an impossible claim and fails to acknowledge the subjectivity of the researcher' (Bravette, 1996: 7). Transparency about my position, agenda and research methods can ensure validity, so I adopted a reflexive approach, which explores 'the ways in which a researcher's involvement with a particular study influences, acts upon and informs the research' (Nightingale and Cromby, 1999: 228).

Asher (2001) suggests that by documenting minoritized voices, researchers can create alternative discourses that challenge the domination of a 'knowledge' that serves to perpetuate inequalities. Like hooks and West (1991), she emphasizes the political role of black academics in using their own agency to create new knowledge, with a focus on anti-oppression and stimulating change. It was with these objectives in mind that I elected to engage interviewees in discussions about their lived experiences, of their careers and education.

It is difficult to ignore professionally what you experience personally (Asher, 2001) and in my experience of research, the personal and the political are closely interconnected. As a black graduate myself, I have brought my own insights and experiences of racism, elitism and sexism to the research process and these undeniably influenced my understanding and interpretation of the data. Recording and reflecting on my activities in a research diary were invaluable for the reflexive process and the analysis.

Researchers such as hooks (1989) have commented on the significance of race research being carried out from a black perspective and highlighted the benefit of research in which the researcher shares a similar ethnic background to the researched. Undoubtedly, my 'insider' status as a black graduate who had gone through the same educational system as the participants aided communication and enhanced our ability to discuss sensitive issues relating to race and ethnicity in education. This, combined with my experience of research and teaching in education, afforded me the valuable perspective of a 'situated knower' (Collins, 2000) or an 'outsider within' (Collins, 1986). I acknowledge that a researcher from a different background may well have drawn different conclusions from the data, but as the research aimed to give voice to the perspectives of the research subjects, I consider my proximity to them an asset in the research process.

## Ethical issues

All interviewee names have been changed to guarantee confidentiality in the transcripts and the analysis. Similarly, the names of employers and institutions have been altered where details of sensitive issues were revealed.

# Theoretical framework

The theoretical framework draws on reproduction theory, critical race theory, black feminist theory and intersectionality in order to analyse the experiences of black graduates in their education and careers.

## *Reproduction theory*

Among cultural reproduction theorists, Bourdieu's work on the interplay between 'habitus' and 'capital' is particularly influential. Bourdieu illustrates how the norms of behaviour that set the standards within education are based on the dominant group's (i.e. middle/ruling class) values and thus give children from those backgrounds a distinct advantage. Habitus is an individual's 'way of being', acquired through socialization, and capitals are the resources, both real and symbolic, that the individual can call upon as recognition tools. A middle-class habitus aids success in the educational system, because 'when habitus encounters a social world of which it is the product, it is like a "fish in water": it does not feel the weight of the water, and it takes the world about itself for granted' (Bourdieu and Wacquant, 1992: 127).

In addition, all individuals have access to resources of economic, social, cultural and symbolic capital, but their value varies according to how close they are to those legitimated by the dominant group. The cumulative effect is that middle/ruling-class habitus and capital lead to greater privilege because of what the individual has (capital) and who the individual is (values, tastes and ways of being). Bourdieu provides a useful mechanism for comprehending the ways that inequality is perpetuated and power is maintained among certain groups. Access to power is easiest for those who already have it, and gaining power requires acceptance from those who already have it. New capital is not easily acquired, nor is it readily recognized. Instead, it is subject to stringent tests that appear more severe than those adhered to even by the judges themselves.

Bourdieu's work centres on culture and is useful for explaining class inequalities. Critical race theory, black feminist theory and intersectionality align closely to cultural reproduction theories and recognize the value in applying them alongside more nuanced explanations of how societal structures perpetuate race and gender inequalities.

## *Critical race theory*

Critical race theory offers a way to analyse and critique educational research and practice (Ladson-Billings, 2005) and make sense of ongoing racial inequality in educational experiences and career outcomes.

Race is central to critical race theory and is understood to be inextricably linked to other forms of structural inequity such as class and gender. The theory suggests that traditional claims of meritocracy, neutrality, objectivity and colour blindness are generally a form of camouflage for the self-interest, power and privilege of dominant groups (Yosso, 2005). Hence, although education could emancipate and empower, it frequently serves to oppress and marginalize. Critical race theory acknowledges that the experiential knowledge of minoritized people is essential to understanding how racism operates. It suggests that racism is the norm, and thus the 'taken-for-granted routine privileging of white interests that goes unremarked in the political mainstream' (Gillborn, 2005: 485) is the most subtle and harmful form of institutional racism. Institutionalized racism appears normal, because it is embedded in the system.

Yosso (2005) combines critical race theory with an adaptation of Bourdieu's theory of capitals in order to demonstrate the positive role of social and cultural capital in minoritized communities. She identifies a range of capitals that are passed on through these families and communities and then used to survive and resist macro and micro forms of oppression. By centring the black experience and acknowledging the cultural knowledge, skills, abilities and contacts that minoritized people possess, her concept of 'community cultural wealth' transforms our knowledge and understanding of how minoritized students achieve educationally.

### Black feminist theory

Black feminism emerged out of the failure of the women's liberation movement to address issues of race adequately, and the failure of the black liberation movement to address issues of gender adequately. With black women also traditionally positioned among the poorer working class, black feminism has the explicit agenda of examining race, class and gender in conjunction with each other to gain an understanding of the different forms of oppression. In black feminism, 'black' is used as an inclusive term for minoritized women.

During the third wave of feminism in the 1980s and 1990s, a growing body of black academics, including bell hooks, Patricia Hill Collins and Heidi Mirza, began to represent black women's perspectives within the feminist literature, with education featuring as a key topic. hooks (1994) explores how the prevalence of white, middle-class values in education marginalizes and silences black and working-class students in the classroom, casting them as 'other' and perpetuating forms of dominance.

In contrast, a truly multicultural, anti-racist, inclusive, diverse or decolonized (~~Coleman~~, 2015) curriculum (I use these terms interchangeably throughout the book) would consistently include a range of African and Asian heritage cultures, authors, art, history and scientists in all subject areas. It would provide a more holistic worldview that acknowledges contributions of minoritized cultures to society. The need for such a curriculum reverberates throughout the black feminist literature. Yet, a multicultural curriculum in British schools, colleges and universities is sporadic, which perpetuates the underlying problem of tacitly reinforcing racist, Eurocentric epistemology. For hooks (1994), the reluctance of education policy makers and practitioners to adopt multiculturalism that goes beyond the tokenism of one class at the end of a course is symptomatic of 'the fear that any de-centering of Western civilizations, of the white male canon, is really an act of cultural genocide' (hooks, 1994: 32).

Inevitably, gender is a key element of a black feminist perspective on education and there are marked gender differences in attainment among black learners. As individuals interact within their social setting they learn to 'perform' gender (Butler, 1990), but '[n]ot all performances of gender are equal: some carry more weight and power than others' (Archer and Francis, 2007: 32). Importantly, gendering produces different experiences according to its interconnection with race and class. The theory of intersectionality, thus, explores how combinations of race, class and gender dis/advantage and produce different outcomes. Morris (2007) expounds:

> An intersectional approach examines 'the ways in which gender is racialized and race is gendered' (Glenn, 2002). Race alters the very meaning and impact of gender and gender alters the very meaning and impact of race.
>
> (Morris, 2007: 491–2)

## Intersectionality

Kimberlé Crenshaw (1991) first used the term 'intersectionality' to argue that ignoring the ways that different elements of our identity, such as race, class, gender and sexuality intersect can lead to minoritized women falling between the cracks of the feminist and anti-racist movements, thereby creating further marginalization. She concludes that identity politics could be an empowering way for marginalized people to join forces in the pursuit of social justice, particularly if they move away from an essentialist view of group members – for example, 'women' means white women, or 'black' means black men. She argues that solidarity can be achieved by acknowledging intra-group differences and understanding how those different combinations of the various elements of identity create different experiences of oppression. For instance, a straight, working class, black woman's experience of gender oppression would differ from that of a straight, working class, white woman and would also differ from a gay, working class, black woman. Intersectionality thus 'emphasizes that different dimensions of social life cannot be separated out into discrete and pure strands' (Brah and Phoenix, 2004: 76).

As Yosso (2005) notes, many theories that deal with race or class or gender have blind spots that serve to create a hierarchy of oppressions. In contrast, intersectionality is all-encompassing in terms of its inclusive nature and its premise that oppression is neither simple nor experienced in one single way. Instead, it is experienced in multiple ways and every combination must be theorized and addressed to challenge injustice.

By drawing on this and other relevant literature, this book explores how black graduates in the UK experience the intersection of race, class and gender in their careers and educational journeys.

## Outline of the book

In grappling with the research questions, the rest of this book is organized into five chapters.

In Chapter 2, I present the common themes that emerged regarding school experiences. The dominant trend among my participants was that they achieved far less than their full potential during their secondary school education and I examine the reasons they identified for this. Negative racial stereotyping was a dominant theme. For girls this was transmitted predominantly through school teachers' low expectations and for boys through conflict between peer groups and teachers. I explore strategies for improving conditions for black pupils by increasing the diversity of school teaching staff and the school curriculum. Bourdieu's concept of cultural capital is utilized to analyse how social class and cultural difference can affect black parents' ability to challenge injustices and secure a good education for their children.

Chapter 3 discusses the motivations and journeys of participants in my study from the time that they left compulsory schooling until their entry into higher education. Most spent time in post-compulsory education compensating for their lack of school leaving qualifications. The participants journeyed through a range of transitions and their paths were characterized by serendipity and stepping stones. Minoritized and anti-racist practitioners acted as catalysts and this highlights the importance of ensuring that role models of this kind are in key positions where they can have a positive influence on black students' achievement. Motivations to study centred primarily on parental expectations and social mobility. However, the pleasure of studying also emerged as an influential factor, particularly for the women. Finally in this chapter, I delve into the impact of race and class dynamics in graduates' choices of higher education institutions.

Most participants saw the higher education experience as a positive and worthwhile endeavour, which was in sharp contrast to their experiences of school. The lack of diversity in higher education was the main downside and Chapter 4 explores the strategies used for coping with this. Microaggressions were confirmed as a source of racism and respondents used emotional withdrawal to minimize the disruption caused by poor relationships with some of their predominantly white lecturers. The consensus among these graduates was that a more multicultural curriculum was needed. Some challenged the Eurocentric bias by presenting a black perspective in their university work whenever possible, but there was a degree of risk associated with this strategy.

On entry to higher education, several participants expressed concerns about fitting in and about their own academic ability. These insecurities are deconstructed in light of the literature on social class and race in higher education. Black support networks played an important role in overcoming these anxieties.

The majority of participants progressed to postgraduate study and here a gender dynamic became evident through the prevalence of women continuing their studies. However, class-related and gender-related issues tempered the women's inclinations towards PhD study. Clearly, black women could be encouraged into academic careers through implementation of policies that break down these barriers and create clearer pathways between studying at master's degree level and embarking on academic careers. The presence of more black women in academic roles would redress the under-representation of minoritized staff and the under-representation of women in higher education.

Chapter 5 makes an important contribution to the literature by analysing the professional lives of black graduates in the UK, which still remains relatively uncharted territory. Narratives about career paths suggest a bitter-sweet combination of success in gaining entry to professions, and frustration at battling against oppressive organizational structures. There is a strong sense that organizational structures serve to constrain rather than develop black graduates in their professional careers and this is explored through the theoretical lens of 'glass ceilings' and 'sticky floors'.

All of the participants embarked on professional careers in their chosen fields. Their choice of direction tied in with three themes: public sector careers, entrepreneurialism and community service. I discuss the impact that primary responsibility for home and family continues to have on the professional careers of mothers.

In Chapter 6, I conclude by outlining how the structuring effects of race, class and gender were typically experienced by these black graduates via the frustrations of unfulfilled potential in school, long journeys through post-compulsory education, microaggressions in higher education and a general lack of diversity in staffing and curriculum throughout the education system. I go on to demonstrate how, despite their academic achievements, participants' outsider status frequently created obstacles to their career progression.

The focus then shifts to the resources on which these black graduates were able to draw in order to succeed. It was largely the minoritized and anti-racist educators, and black social capital in the form of black support networks, that were key enhancers of the experience of post-compulsory and higher education. In careers, entrepreneurialism was identified as an alternative to unfriendly structures in organizations. The ways that participants sought to use their skills and experiences to challenge the structuring effects of race, class and gender suggest a process of 'conscientization' (Freire, 1996), an 'awakening political consciousness' (Bravette, 1996: 3). This was reflected in their career orientations, in their voluntary work and in their aspirations to combine entrepreneurial endeavours with community service.

Finally, I summarize the key policy implications and directions for future research and include an examination of the benefits of supporting black graduates in developing community-oriented enterprises.

## Conclusion

This chapter has provided an introduction to the book, outlining its purpose and contribution to the field. I have discussed the rationale for the research, including the political backdrop of education policy relating to widening participation and social inclusion. I also explored the need for more research from a black perspective that examines the socio-economic conditions affecting black learners in their education and careers. Research aims, research questions and the structure of the book were outlined. Subsequent chapters will analyse the main findings of the research based on the experiences of the ten graduate interviewees.

# Notes

[1] During the 1990s the term 'Black' or 'black' was used politically as an inclusive term for all non-whites, who faced oppression on the common grounds of race. However, throughout this book, except where otherwise stated, the term 'black' is used to refer to people who are physically recognizably of African heritage (e.g. African, African-Caribbean, African-American).

[2] All non-white ethnicities (e.g. African, African-Caribbean, Indian, Chinese, dual heritage).

*Chapter 2*

# Unfulfilled potential: School experiences

There is a silent catastrophe happening in Britain's schools in the way they continue to fail black British children.

(Diane Abbott, Labour MP, 2002)

## Introduction

In this chapter I discuss school experiences. Although the participants were in school some time ago, their experiences warrant examining, because secondary school represents a particularly low point in their educational journeys and the negative consequences reach far into their futures. Most participants did not achieve their full potential in secondary school. The reasons they identified resonate with literature on race, class and gender in schools today (e.g. Rollock *et al.*, 2015) and continue to affect the educational performance of black children in the UK.

Their school trajectories demonstrate how their socio-economic class impeded their access to effective schooling and racism compounded the effects of class. Most participants experienced negative racial stereotyping from teachers, which manifested in low teacher expectations for girls and high levels of conflict for boys. Diversity is a feature of the education agenda (Education Commission, 2004), so I discuss the positive influence of minoritized and anti-racist teachers, and of multicultural curricula. As parental involvement is instrumental in the school process (Desforges and Abouchaar, 2003), I also examine the attitudes of participants' parents. I conclude with a summary of the main findings.

## The typical school trajectory

The government's current preoccupation with educational achievement is characterized by an emphasis on examination passes (Archer and Francis, 2007). League tables have created benchmarks of success based on children attaining five GCSE passes at grades A* to C at school leaving age. At the same time, diversity and inclusion are on the agenda of educational institutions seeking to address inequality (DfES, 2003). Nonetheless, attainment levels among cohorts of minoritized and African-Caribbean students have remained below average (DfES, 2003) and although the gap has narrowed, it has not closed up (EHRC, 2015). So it is no surprise that only two of the graduates I interviewed enjoyed school success as defined by government policy.

Elaine's and Leroy's school success was in stark contrast with the typical school trajectory of the other eight participants. Negative experiences of secondary school were common and narratives were littered with references to declining grades and unfulfilled potential. This reflects the DfES (2003) finding that:

> evidence from LEAs [local education authorities] and from the Ofsted review of research shows that the academic achievement of African Caribbean pupils is often higher at Key Stage 1 than other groups and then attainment gradually declines relative to other groups and is amongst the lowest at Key Stage 4.
>
> (DfES, 2003: 3)

Teachers' low expectations and stereotyping lead to the low assessment of black pupils' ability on internally graded assessments, until external marking begins at age 14 and their grades increase in relation to their white peers (Burgess and Greaves, 2009). Ability grouping then caps students' attainment, as they are prepared and entered for lower-tier examinations.

Socio-economic class is a key indicator of educational success (Hutchinson *et al.*, 2011) and achievement can vary considerably depending on the type of school attended. Working-class children who attend poorly resourced inner city schools tend to fare worst (Reay, 2001). Post-war mass immigration from the former British colonies positioned most first-generation African-Caribbean migrants firmly among the British working classes in terms of their access to jobs, housing and education (Coard, 1971). Consequently, African-Caribbean children are still largely concentrated in inner city schools (Rhamie and Hallam, 2002) and this was the case among my research participants. All attended state secondary schools, none of which was selective. When reflecting on the standard of education offered by their schools, several felt that there had generally been insufficient emphasis on academic achievement:

> I don't know why, but I often think about my schooling. I think it's because the people I socialize with nowadays, a lot of them had a damn good education ... And I messed up with school ...

> And I always think that if I'd gone to a better school ... I would
> have done better.
>
> (Neil, IT trainer)

However, the complexity of issues that affect black children go beyond
social class (Education Commission, 2004) and 'the correlation between
class indicators and attainment is not as strong for Black Caribbean and
Black African pupils as for white ethnic groups' (DfES, 2003: 7). As a group,
black boys from middle-class backgrounds achieve less well than working-
class boys from other backgrounds (Education Commission, 2004) and
when compared with girls from the same schools and circumstances, black
girls perform better than their white counterparts, although not as well as
Asian and Chinese girls (Mirza, 2005).

Even in the least successful schools, some children of high academic
ability achieve well. This raises the question: why were the research
participants, who had the ability to subsequently graduate from university,
unable to achieve in school? The most fundamental hindrance to emerge
from their narratives was poor teacher–student relationships. While there
was significant overlap across the sexes, my main observation is that teachers
had low expectations of girls and conflictual relationships with boys.

## Schooling the girls

Good teacher–student relationships and high teacher expectations are
of paramount importance for a child's academic success. hooks (1994)
extols the benefits of teachers being genuinely concerned for the children
in their care. For the participants, good teacher–student relationships
were characterized by teachers being caring, supportive and encouraging.
Michelle described the profound impact of one teacher's belief in her:

> I had Mr S*. I wish I could hunt him down and find out where
> he is because he was an excellent teacher. He said to me that you
> can do anything you want to do. Anything you set your mind to
> do, you can do it ... And I believed him. And I don't think I could
> have had a more important statement given to me at that time.
> And when I left primary school I had this in my mind.
>
> (Michelle, teacher)

However, high teacher expectations were rare and there were very few
examples of teachers actively encouraging these students. Elaine and
Michelle were the only interviewees whose teachers expected them to go to
university. Nora highlighted the vast difference between what she achieved

in school and what she achieved a few years later. She explained the reasons for her poor school outcomes:

> Low expectations. That is just so obvious now, because how could I go through a whole schooling and not really achieve anything in terms of my capability; and then leave school and get three A levels at A grade? I mean it just shows that at school, what did they do with me? They had no expectations of my capability. So, that was a big barrier ... So, when they talk about low expectations that is so real for me.
>
> (Nora, headteacher)

Teachers systematically place African-Caribbean children in lower ability groups (Mac an Ghaill, 1988; Mirza, 1992). Participants recounted examples of unchallenging classwork, lack of encouragement, and teachers blatantly trying to undermine their aspirations despite clear evidence of their ability. Alison's teachers advised her that she did not 'need' high-status qualifications and entered her for lower ones. In the same vein, Michelle's teacher strongly advised her against selecting the sciences that she excelled in for her options and then tried to demote her to a lower-ability set. Michelle described herself as a pupil who was always 'well behaved' and worked hard 'because I knew that was where I could achieve'. Nevertheless:

> I had these exams and I think the lowest I got was the fifth highest in the class for sciences ... I was in the top for everything ... and Science was the easiest [for me] ... and I said to [the teacher] that I was going to take three sciences and she said, 'Three sciences is almost impossible to pass. You will never do it.' I just ignored her and decided I was going to do three sciences ... and out of all the children in my class she came to me and said, 'We're going to put you down a group.' So I was a child on my own and these two teachers came to me and told me that they were going to put me down a group. And I said, 'No! Why would you do that? These are my exam results. How can you basically justify doing that?' ... I was so furious that [my mum] went up to the school and spoke to the Head [and after that] they left me in that top group ... And then I moved up to my High School and it went on the report that you got, so they put me in the CSE[1] group and my [black] friend was with me as well. And she said, 'We're not supposed to be in this group!' And they said, 'Well, you're here now and we've got an exam come Christmas [and if you] do well

you can move up.' The work that they gave us was just so easy that it didn't even take us half the time. We spent most of the time talking to the Chemistry teacher and our Physics teacher ... Our grades were easily the highest in the class, [but] by the time we moved up the other students stigmatized us, because as far as they were concerned we were really CSE students. And that's how the teachers spoke of us as well ... Funnily enough, the O levels that I got straight away, even though I didn't really revise that much for them, were the science O levels. And if I had listened to that woman I wouldn't have really got any.

(Michelle, teacher)

This account demonstrates the power some teachers exert, and how it can ultimately restrict black children's life choices. From her position as a teacher now, Michelle reflects on her unfair treatment and how bold it was for her, aged 12, to fight against the decision of her teacher and head of science. Her mother hampered their efforts to demote Michelle when she successfully challenged them and the headteacher agreed that she remain in the top class. But the class teacher's report to the next school ensured that Michelle went into a lower set after transition. Michelle and her friend, who was also black, recognized the injustice and used their power of agency to work hard and prove their suitability for the higher set. They were finally moved up, only to find that in addition to the difficulties of adjusting to a different syllabus and class, they faced the stigma among their peers of coming up from a lower set. This continual battle to prove oneself in the face of a constant barrage of negativity would undermine most children's confidence in their academic ability. Michelle's decision to ignore the teacher's advice in terms of subject choice, and her success in those particular subjects, correspond with Mac an Ghaill's (1988) finding that many successful black students disregard teacher assessments of their ability.

Eve had a similar experience. Teachers placed her in CSE groups and she had to prove herself capable of sitting O levels. Again, all of those in her class who were promoted to higher sets were minoritized students. Although it is encouraging that teachers eventually promoted them, it is an indictment of the school as an institution that systematically impedes the academic attainment of black pupils, instead of actively encouraging and developing their talents. Teachers, intentionally or unintentionally, racially stereotype black children as low achievers and students have to be very brave to constantly fight the system and struggle with the additional and unnecessary burdens put upon them. As a result of low teacher expectations, the participants said that time was wasted in lessons where the work was well beneath their capabilities and offered absolutely no academic development.

Low teacher expectations and negative racial stereotyping can have a detrimental effect on the future of African-Caribbean children. Their career aspirations are assessed as unrealistically high (Mirza, 1992) and careers advice tends to reinforce existing stereotypes (Hutchinson *et al.*, 2011). Interviewees generally felt that careers advice was poor and Alison expressed her frustration at the advice she received in spite of her aspirations to a professional career:

> They knew [what] I wanted ... but they don't think you will ... I did feel with the O levels and the A levels it was ... battling with the teachers.
>
> (Alison, higher education (HE) lecturer)

From the age of 8, Eve wanted to be a hairdresser. She described her experience of applying for a popular hairdressing course at college:

> I had a careers interview and my mum came with me and it was absolutely dreadful. I told [the careers teacher] what I wanted to do and he said, 'Why are you applying for the full-time hairdressing course? Why don't you be an apprentice?' And I said, 'Well, I just feel that if I'm going to study this as a career I'd like to learn everything about it and start from scratch.' And he said 'Well, you won't get into [the prestigious college].' He didn't say, 'Well, try and apply ... go for it.' He said, 'You *will not* get in.' And as a 15-year-old I remember sitting there and I could feel the tears filling up, because it was like suddenly all my hopes and dreams ... and there's this man in authority telling me that I wouldn't get a place. So I said, 'Why?' And he said, 'Well, it's very, very competitive.' So of course *I* wouldn't get in. So I said, 'Well, have you looked at my grades and noted what the teachers are predicting?' And he said, 'Oh well yes, they're fine, but you won't get in.' ... I remember even back then being quite strong ... My mum said, 'What would [you] like to do then?' Because [she] felt disappointed for me. I said, 'Well, if I don't get on to do the full-time course I won't bother. I'll just do something else.' And I just said to Mum, 'Come on. Let's go.' And so we went ... but my mum was very quiet, because it's like a mentality of the teachers having the power ... So Mum didn't really ask him anything.
>
> (Eve, entrepreneur/teacher)

When Eve applied and the college turned her down, it seemed to confirm the careers teacher's negative assumption. She felt crushed. However, a year later, she was encouraged to re-apply by a particularly good careers teacher and discovered that there was no apparent reason for the rejection of her first application:

I applied straight from school to [the prestigious] college to do hairdressing and ... there were no black people [there] ... I still applied, but then I didn't get in the first time; which was like 'Oh my God, [the careers teacher] was right, no matter how horrible he was!' And I was really, really gutted. It threw me completely ... So I felt like I was just going aimlessly with the wind ... I started to do A level Chemistry, but my heart was never in it ... And then I had another careers interview [and] I decided not to mention hairdressing, because I just felt it was probably a sign that I wasn't meant to go ahead with hairdressing. And so I spent an hour with this careers officer who was really nice and eventually she said, 'We've gone through nearly every possible career and everything you've said is fine ... We've just spent an hour and I'm none the wiser really. Where do we go from here?' And then right at the end she said, 'Is there something that you've always wanted to do?' She'd never asked that question [before]. And I laughed and I said, 'Well, I wasn't going to mention it at all, because I think I'm probably not meant to do it, but I've always wanted to do hairdressing and I applied and didn't get in.' She said, 'Oh my God! Don't be daft ... Apply again. Don't be defeated.' She was really positive ... I went through the same test and [was selected for] an interview. So this is quite intriguing, because I didn't get an interview the first time, but the second time I did. And at this interview I had two teachers ... and they said, 'We noticed you applied before and you didn't get in. Do you know why?' And *they* were asking *me* why! I said, 'Well, I don't know,' and they said, 'We're just shocked that you didn't get in the first time.' And they looked at each other and I've always thought 'What were they thinking?' Because a week after, I was firmly accepted on the course. No hassle at all. So I don't know what it was about the year before ... There were 37 that had made it out of four hundred people [and] me and a guy were the only black people on the course. There weren't any other either mixed raced or Asian ... And as soon as I started I loved it and I just knew that 'Yes, I'm happy in this.' And I think because of it I did really well.

(Eve, entrepreneur/teacher)

Eve went on to be a model student, winning awards, representing the college and having newspaper articles written about her. Clearly, she was very able. She also went on to start her own successful hairdressing business at age 21, which she still operates on a part-time basis. Mirza (1992) and Alison Allen (1998) find that black students' expectations are generally lowered by careers advisers and Eve's first careers interview exemplifies this. Her story demonstrates the accumulation of obstacles that hinder the academic progress of black children, shaping their lives and reproducing inequalities. Her articulation of her emotions conveys the depth of impact that teacher prejudices can have on a child's self-belief resulting in lost dreams. Despite her predicted high grades, the teacher considered it unrealistic for Eve to apply to the best college course in the region so he directed her to the apprenticeship, which offered a lower-status qualification. His patronizing attitude is characteristic of inherent negative racial stereotyping. Her mother, although disappointed for Eve, was ill equipped to challenge the teacher's flawed assumptions or act on her daughter's behalf. (I discuss parental involvement later.) The mysterious rejection of Eve's initial application raises unanswered questions about the reference and the college recruitment process. The persistence of the second careers teacher again illustrates the importance of the caring professional, whose genuine concern makes a difference. Without it, Eve would have undoubtedly abandoned the pursuit of her goal.

Channer (1995) identifies a pattern in which successful African-Caribbean students may encounter a 'benevolent individual' who assists with careers or academic advice and compensates for the shortcomings in the system, but suggests that for many 'having the academic ability [is] not enough' (Channer, 1995: 93). In Eve's case, the influence of a benevolent individual who guided her through the system was a catalyst and key determinant of her success.

Four of the five female graduates left school with only two or three O level passes. It is apparent that the school system failed to support the fulfilment of their potential.

### Schooling the boys

Concern about the 'underachievement' of boys in relation to girls has been the driving force behind the growing body of literature on working-class and black masculinities in education (e.g. Graham and Robinson, 2004;

Odih, 2002; Reay, 2002; Skelton, 2001). Wright *et al.* (1998) contend that education policy aligns the elements required to succeed in education with middle-class masculinities. In contrast, working-class masculinities are less acceptable and black masculinities wholly unacceptable. They conclude that 'it is race which determines how gender is experienced' (Wright *et al.*, 1998: 79).

Whereas the women in this research identified low teacher expectations as the most significant factor, the men recounted similar experiences, but to a lesser degree. Some felt that teachers held them back educationally and others saw it more as a lack of encouragement. Accordingly, they assumed part of the responsibility for not seizing the educational opportunity:

> I was O level standard from day one, but wasn't given the opportunity to go into that group. And I never asked for it. And I didn't realize that it was that important at the time. The opportunities [weren't] laid on the table, like they should have been; like teachers should want to do that. So, I went through that system. I've got no resentment ... it was an excellent learning experience for me ... because I know that any child I've got and all my nephews now, they won't be going through that again. It will be completely different, because I'm challenging it ... And if I'm not satisfied I'm taking it further ... So I try to deal with injustice at school. [I] left with no qualifications.
>
> (Dean, youth worker)

Negative racial stereotyping on the part of teachers leads them to perceive black children, in particular boys, as a threat (Mac an Ghaill, 1988; Bryan *et al.*, 1985). As a consequence, black children are 'disproportionately controlled and criticised' (Gillborn 1998: 14). Teacher–student relationships play an integral role in exclusions (Pomeroy, 1999) and there is a long history of schools excluding black children more frequently than white children (Wright *et al.*, 1998; EHRC, 2015). Disproportionate numbers of black children also continue to be categorized as having special educational needs (Coard, 1971; Richardson, 2005).

A number of the men and women in the research noted that hostile teacher–student relationships led to a lack of understanding and the unfair treatment of black students. Being perceived as a threat was not gender specific, but was accentuated for boys. Sewell (1997) notes that the media and wider society stereotypically portray black males as a threat that needs to be controlled. This shapes the way teachers perceive them and even the way they see themselves.

In his seminal research, Mac an Ghaill (1988) analysed teacher interactions with peer groups of black and Asian schoolboys and observed that it was the racialized interpretations of behaviour, rather than the behaviour itself, that led to conflict between teachers and black boys. He notes that teachers held different racial stereotypes, viewing black boys in behavioural terms and Asian boys in terms of technical ability. This stereotyping allowed no room for academically successful black boys, who were resented and usually put down to lower grades. By contrast, Asian boys, with their 'technical problems' were placed in higher sets.

Sean encapsulated this issue in his relationship with his teachers:

> Some teachers found me and some of my friends quite intimidating. And I don't know if that's a reflection of why black youths don't engage in the education system as much. So I had some bad experiences with some teachers where the teachers were downright unfair, which affected my ability to work within the class ... And I think sometimes it's a challenge thing, it's a challenge to your manhood. Even though you're still a boy, you have a sense of pride. And sometimes it's a challenge to that.
>
> (Sean, housing advice manager)

As boys developing their masculine identities, my participants construed being 'shamed' by teachers in front of their peers as a very real issue. So when teachers used public humiliation to control a situation, they protected their self-respect through confrontation – for example, answering back – rather than submission. Sewell (1997) identified this problem in his research and found that boys simply wanted teachers to treat them with respect but that teachers interpreted this as subversive. Consequently, conflicts arose between black boys and their teachers due to lack of respect on the teachers' part – sometimes including racist comments – and insubordination on the boys' part.

The accentuated fear of black boys diverts attention from the aggression that is directed at them. Dean gave an example of an incident of racial abuse, where a teacher chose to ignore the initial act of aggression and focused on punishing the retaliation:

> A lot of the teachers need to be getting ... appropriate training, because they're working with a lot of black men and I think they're scared ... throughout the system [and] especially at schools ... My nephew was verbally, racially assaulted and when he hit this guy, they ... were going to put on his file that he assaulted this guy.

> And his parents said, 'Be careful how you use the word assault, because it tends to stay with you throughout your career. So you need to rephrase that.' Fortunately, they did. And [his parents] said, 'You need to be talking about this racial abuse. How are you going to handle that?' [The teachers] chose not to see the racial abuse part, but they wanted to concentrate on the assault part. I think a lot of them feel threatened and they don't know how to deal with it, so they think the best thing is to exclude. And to exclude is like that downward cycle of destruction.
>
> (Dean, youth worker)

Although I do not condone fighting in the playground, I must acknowledge that toughness is one of the ways in which boys maintain their self-respect and respect among their peers (Reay, 2002). Dean's example demonstrates how racial abuse can trigger a confrontation and how retaliation can lead to serious consequences for the victim of racism. Gillborn (1998) notes that teachers often respond inappropriately to racist slurs and attacks in school, minimizing them and not recognizing them as bullying. The Department for Education and Skills (DfES, 2003) found that a declared approach against racism in the school raises the achievement of minoritized students. It conveys the message that schools will not tolerate racism and protects minoritized students with an effective alternative that leaves their dignity intact.

Showing respect is an important element in African-Caribbean male culture and even the youngest boy is often greeted by older men as 'big man' as a mark of respect. Both of the examples above highlight how, in defending their male pride, black boys may challenge injustice in inappropriate ways and exacerbate situations. Sewell (1997) identified that, while society constructs 'whiteness' around the concept of privilege, for many black boys constructions of 'blackness' revolve around rebelliousness towards a hostile system. He outlines conflict resolution techniques to equip black (and white) boys with alternative strategies to diffuse conflict. He also suggests that a process of re-education could enable black boys to reject the negative stereotypes and internalized racism that they sometimes reinforce within their peer groups, and understand how these perpetuate their own oppression.

During my research male interviewees identified their involvement in peer groups as a source of perpetual conflict with teachers and a root cause of their underachievement in school:

In my class there were really a lot of 'mess about' children. There were only a few of us who worked and they were mainly girls. So they carried on as girls do, but I just was mixed up in the wrong crowd. I started in the top groups and by the fifth year I was sliding and sliding and I was only doing four O levels by the time I got to [school leaving age]. And that was my fault, my own doing. And I always think that if I'd gone to a better school, because of peer pressure again, I would have done better.

(Neil, IT trainer)

It is interesting that when Neil contrasts the progression of his female peers with his own academic decline, he links it to his choice of friendship group. This highlights how working-class and black masculinities can be at odds with school achievement. Consequently, male participants blamed their poor school outcomes not only on bad teacher–student relationships, but also on their own lack of interest and motivation to learn. Most also noted that there was very little encouragement in academic subjects, but plenty of encouragement for sports. This conforms to the popular image of black male sporting prowess, which feeds into another racial stereotype. When asked what contributed to his school leaving results, Zac replied:

I can't really blame [the teachers] as such, but I wasn't really pushed or encouraged from them at all. The encouragement really was just for sports ... I remember our school was one of the best at basketball and the basketball team was literally 80–90 per cent black. And all my mates, we used to go around thrashing all the other schools. I can remember on several occasions, members being left off detention because there was a game; so, kind of given a bligh [let off] through the sports. But if I was to think back at the subjects, there was no major encouragement for those ... I think, being fair to them, they probably encouraged us to do the sports, because we were good at it. Obviously, we were skilled in football, basketball ... So, at least they were helping us through that ... At the same time, you need all the other things as well and that push was not there.

(Zac, entrepreneur)

Sewell (1997) contends that due to the heightened influence of black music, dress, sports and sexuality in popular youth culture, black boys enjoy increased admiration and respect from their peers and 'the way in which the students adopt teacher stereotypes as part of their own reputation within the peer-group is one example of how racism takes on a life of its own' (Sewell, 1997: 47). He asserts:

> The peer group imposed both positive and negative influences; it was at once a cauldron of new vibrant Black culture, vital to the creation of an African-Caribbean identity in a hostile world, and a trap into a perception of Black boys as a force only of rebellion and never of conformity and creativity.
>
> (Sewell, 1997: 219)

Osborne (2001) indicates that black boys are subject to negative racial stereotyping long before their achievement begins to decline. This heightens their anxiety about their academic ability and a process of 'academic disidentification' sets in motion. Academic disidentification is the 'detaching of self-esteem from academic outcomes' (Osborne, 2001: 49) and is part of a defence mechanism adopted by the ego to protect itself. In order to maintain self-esteem, people are inclined to value activities that people expect them to excel in and to devalue activities in which people expect them to fail. The individual's aspirations conform to others' expectations. Working-class 'laddishness' and rejection of academics in school is similarly associated with protection of self-worth (Jackson, 2002).

Male participants in this research were inclined towards sporting prowess and became disassociated from academic success by themselves and by others. They played out the self-fulfilling prophecy of academic underachievement. Four of these five male graduates left school without any O level passes.

## Diversity in schools

One of the most effective strategies for tackling negative racial stereotyping and raising achievement for minoritized pupils is increasing the presence of minoritized (Education Commission, 2004) and anti-racist teachers in schools (Arbouin, 1989).

Teachers provide the main interface with the school system and thus received much of the criticism relating to negative school experiences in the participants' narratives. Teachers' lack of awareness of cultural diversity and their negative racial stereotyping of black pupils was the root of the problem. It is vital, therefore, that teachers understand the nature and effects of racial stereotyping and learn to respect non-Western cultures.

Wright *et al.* (2007) use Fanon's (1986) concept of 'black skin, white masks' to demonstrate that the presence of black educators in racist institutions does not necessarily equate to diversity, because they too may adopt white norms of behaviour in order to bypass institutional barriers and gain entry. Applying this to the school context, it follows that black skin does not guarantee an anti-racist teacher. That said, my participants who encountered black teachers were hugely positive about their influence, citing cases of their fair treatment of black pupils and the guidance and support they offered.

Michelle recalled teachers placing her in a set below her ability. A Caribbean teacher, who knew this was unfair, took a special interest in ensuring that Michelle was moved to the higher set:

> There were thirty children ... four [were black] in that class. We had a Trinidadian teacher ... When I got there I liked her, because she was nice to me ... What I realize [now is] she was actually coaching us. I think she knew that we all had the ability to be in the top class and there was something else that must have been going on, because at the end of that year only three children moved up and they were all black children ... me and my other two friends. And she was geeing us along and asking us how we were doing and things like that. So I think she made it her business to get us into that top class, because she clearly thought that there was something else going on. But we wouldn't have known as children.
>
> (Michelle, teacher)

For black and working-class students to be fully included in the classroom, teachers must be aware of different cultural codes (hooks, 1994). Michelle, in her capacity as a teacher, reiterated this point in relation to the school where she works now. She noted that some teachers misinterpret African-Caribbean students' behaviour and that, as a black teacher, her cultural understanding neutralizes the negative impact this could have:

> The school is more than 50 per cent black ... but they've got one permanent black teacher, one teacher on a year contract, and me. So the children, I think, are very happy to see another black teacher. And sometimes it's important to be aware of culture ... when they're in school, education still seems to be a very white, middle-class environment and those are the rules, those are the standards, and if that's not what you are actually doing, then you are seen somehow to be deviant. So a lot of the time some of the black children are seen to be deviant. Now to me, I think West Indian culture tends to be a lot louder than European culture,

so the children are being loud, but I don't necessarily see that they're doing anything wrong. If they're not working they're doing something wrong, but if they're being loud they're not doing anything wrong. I know I can look up and I can see my middle-class section at the top ... they're talking, they're chatting, but they're getting on with their work. [The] black section will be talking more loudly, but they're still getting on with their work. Sometimes when I had my teaching assistant in the class he'd be saying, 'Oh, look you're making noise, you're talking loudly, get on with your work,' and they'll turn round and say, 'Well, I've done this and I've done that,' and he'll say, 'Show me.' And they'll show him and then he'll say, 'Alright then.' But I don't think it connects with him that they are doing work, because he'll say the same thing and respond to them the very same way in the next lesson. Because he is white and middle class that isn't his culture and he feels that if you're making lots of noise ... and he can hear you chatting you can't possibly be doing work. But I know that they are, because I'm keeping my eye on them and I've also got something called Ranger where I can see exactly what they're doing on their [computer] screens.

(Michelle, teacher)

Nora, having excelled in her teaching career, became a headteacher in her early thirties. She left school with few qualifications and has dedicated her career to improving the performance of schools with large numbers of black and working-class children. About the difficulties faced by black children that directly contribute to poor school leaving results she said:

It has a lot to do with school; the teachers not understanding the attitudes of the black boys in particular and with that comes low expectations about what they can do. They're not driven as hard as they could be under the right circumstances. They don't want to work for teachers when they don't feel that the teachers like them. That is a big thing. I've witnessed that myself too often. The curriculum isn't really geared towards the black children. There's not a lot in there that they can relate to. For example, I can take a lesson and I can chip in things like say, 'Yeah, and you know when you have your rice and peas on a Sunday' ... and the children's ears will prick up. They'll [think,] 'There's something in there for me. She's teaching *me*.' Whereas they don't get that with the white teachers and that hinders them as well. They're not as motivated on that score.

(Nora, headteacher)

On reflection, the participants felt that the mainstream school curriculum they had experienced was alienating for black people, as there were no black perspectives to it, no genuine multiculturalism. A truly multicultural curriculum would include a diverse range of African and Asian heritage cultures, authors, art, history, mathematicians and scientists in all subject areas, to present a more holistic worldview that acknowledged minoritized people's contributions to society. Introducing a multicultural curriculum is an effective way to build positive identities among minoritized students and combat negative racial stereotyping (Jiwani and Regan, 1998). However, the unanimous opinion of my participants was that they had only been able to develop a positive sense of their identity as a black person in relation to education via their extra-curricular activities. Zac commented:

[There's] a need for change in how we're educated, because we're in a system that doesn't say anything positive about black people.

(Zac, entrepreneur)

It is particularly interesting that those who had become teachers believed that the situation in schools remained largely unchanged since their childhood and stressed the need for the curriculum to reflect the diversity of the school and UK population. Both Channer (1995) and Mac an Ghaill (1988) see the rejection of school as a means for students to maintain self-esteem in an environment that disparages the student's own culture. Participants in my research recognized this antagonism and felt they needed to teach their own children about black contributions to society in order to reinforce their self-esteem and highlight the link between education and their history and culture as African-Caribbean people:

[My son] had to do a project on the Romans and so he did [Lucius] Septimius Severus, a black Roman emperor. And he just had to do a project on Egypt, which is all about black people, but I made sure that he brought the perspective of not just about the mummies and the pyramids ... that everybody would talk about [but also] the development of Chemistry and Astronomy and Sciences and Maths. And he had to do a PowerPoint presentation, so he's not only teaching himself and making himself feel good as a black person, but he's also teaching others. And ... [laughs] they're going to realize that every project this boy does is in relation to black people and how good they are. But that's what I do and that helps me, because he has to do the project anyway and they're going to teach him all about the Vikings and the white [and] European side of things. So I always make sure that he has the black side of things as well.

(Nora, headteacher)

Their concerns, as parents of school-age children, bring me to the issue of their own parents' involvement when they were at school.

## Parental involvement

The fact that African-Caribbean children are falling behind as they progress through compulsory schooling (DfES, 2003) may indicate that they do better in the early years when familial influence is strongest and fare worse as their parents' influence on their education diminishes (Mbandaka, 2004). Parental involvement in the learning process is one of the most important elements of school success (Desforges and Abouchaar, 2003). Many African-Caribbean parents struggle to secure a good education for their children and challenge unfair treatment (McKenley, 2005).

Only one participant in my research had a parent who enjoyed a good relationship with her school and possessed the cultural capital needed to navigate the school system to her child's advantage. Elaine explained her mother's insight and ability to exercise parental choice when selecting her school:

The obvious school for you to go to from where we lived wasn't a very good school, so I went further away [but] if I hadn't had a parent who was a teacher, I [probably wouldn't] have been sent to a different school ... And then we moved to [a village] and ... the major reason was just really to do with schools.

(Elaine, consultant)

It is generally accepted that parents want their children to do well in school and black parents are no exception (McKenley, 2005). However, working-class parents tend to see education as something that happens only at school (Evans, 2006) and African-Caribbean parents often rely on a blind faith in the system (Coard, 1971). The Education Commission (2004) found that African-Caribbean parents fell short in helping their children with their schooling and that 'African Caribbean pupils were least likely of all groups to believe that they received good levels of support and encouragement from home most of the time' (Education Commission, 2004: 8).

Contrary to this suggestion, only one participant felt that his parents did not encourage him educationally. Most received considerable encouragement and family discourses propounded 'education as a key to success'.

For many, practical support came to the fore during post-compulsory education in the form of the time and space to study, without the pressure to seek paid employment and contribute to the family income. However, during compulsory schooling, practical support was a weakness and several participants would have benefitted from far more insight, advice and direction regarding the selection of courses and the resultant career possibilities. The array of comments included:

> I do know that when our parents came they did want us to do better than what they had. But I would add that they didn't necessarily know how to help us to do it. They'd just say, *'Go and read your book!'* But there wasn't like, 'Well, what is it that you're doing?' I don't think that there was that link. But there was definitely from my parents that drive and motivation to get qualifications in something, but it was down to me to choose ... I certainly know that my parents wanted us to succeed educationally, so they supported us through getting A levels at school and degrees.
>
> (Alison, HE lecturer)

Regarding school selection, Michelle stated:

> My mum didn't really do any research, because where she came from in the West Indies the teachers did the best that they could. So as far as she was concerned school was good. So any school was good enough. I don't think that the school that we went to was really good. It was just a place to go and it depended on the teacher you got as to how good your education was.
>
> (Michelle, teacher)

These narratives concur with Coard's (1971) view of African-Caribbean parents as having a blind faith in the system. Based on their knowledge of the Caribbean, parents expected teachers to encourage bright children, whatever their social background, as an investment in the community as a whole. However, such expectations in the British context resulted in parents advising children to do whatever the teacher told them and 'Go learn you book'. This hands-off approach did little to enable children to deal with the challenges of schooling in the UK and meant that when injustices occurred, some of the participants did not involve their parents. Eve described a harrowing incident when she almost drowned and the teacher, who assumed she was playing, hit her. She concluded:

> The teachers had ultimate authority. I don't ever remember going home and telling my mum, because ... in the Caribbean the teachers had quite a high standing ... So if I went home and said that [a teacher] had hit me, then it's likely that my dad or mum would have said, 'Well, what did you do? You must have done something.' And so, in that sense they did have all the power.
>
> (Eve, entrepreneur/teacher)

African-Caribbean parents' belief that the teacher knows best can prove detrimental and put their children in a vulnerable position. Eve saw her parents' reluctance to challenge teachers' authority in terms of their Caribbean background, but it also links to social class. The cultural capital and habitus of middle-class parents give them the confidence and ability to challenge authority. Their language and persona are likely to reflect those of the teacher, leading to mutual respect and greater understanding. They are also more likely to see the school and teacher as providing a service to them and be willing and able to exercise parental choice about their children's schooling. These parents are in a position of relative power and experience a more balanced relationship with teachers. On the other hand, many working-class and Caribbean parents who have not excelled in education may feel inadequate in the school environment and in relation to teaching staff. This can lead to frustration, which can exacerbate the situation; or subservience, which can reduce their assertiveness and ability to advocate successfully on their child's behalf.

During one of our interviews Sean explained how his well-resourced secondary school expelled him and his parents were unable to fight the decision, despite believing it was unwarranted:

Sean:   My experience at [one school] came to an abrupt end [when] an incident occurred and I was [expelled] ... I at the time wanted to move to another school [where] I had friends ... Now that's where I'd say my education took a turn for the worse.

Amanda: What did your parents say about it?

Sean:   They weren't happy about it ... my mum really was involved and she basically said, 'Well, if they've got that sort of attitude knowing that you haven't done it, it's better that you leave, because they've obviously got a negative view of you ...' So we didn't want to appeal the decision or anything. We just thought it's better that we get into another school and that was it.

Amanda:     With hindsight, do you think that was a good idea?

Sean:        No, I don't in hindsight. I lost out really a lot on my education. Because I was on course to do O levels at [that school] and I ended up when I came out of [the other school] with grade 5 or 6 CSEs.

Communications between schools and African-Caribbean parents tend to revolve around issues of behaviour and rarely focus on academic endeavour. As a result, relationships are frequently strained and 'In general Black parents [do] not feel welcome at their children's schools and [are] frustrated at not being able to work in a genuine partnership' (Education Commission, 2004: 9). The experiences of my participants reflect this imbalance, although sometimes their parents were able to negotiate on their behalf and limit the damage caused by unfair teachers. Dean's comments demonstrate this and highlight the influence of class on his parents' different attitudes towards schooling:

My mum's an only child, she comes from quite a well-off family and she had very high standards. That's where our motivations to go to university came from. She was very adamant that you need to go through the education system in order to get something. She had a different attitude from a lot of West Indian parents. Whereas other West Indian parents would listen to what the teacher said at school, my mum would come and question it ... My dad comes from a different background. One of eight children. He wanted to come to England for a better life. He had a different attitude ... But I think both of them together kind of complemented each other ... if it was an injustice my mum was at school like a bullet.

(Dean, youth worker)

The literature identifies tried-and-tested ways forward, such as: (a) greater collaboration between schools and black parents (Education Commission, 2004); (b) more research in the communities and homes of black parents to highlight their viewpoints on parental involvement (McKenley, 2005); and

(c) more outreach initiatives, including parent workshops, to equip African-Caribbean parents to become more actively involved in their children's schooling (Rhamie, 2007). Government funding mechanisms to support education policy that addresses these needs consistently at national level are yet to materialize.

## Conclusions

Black children encounter a mix of race, class and gender dynamics in school. This chapter suggests that social class positioned the majority of the participants in under-resourced inner city schools with relatively low academic standards and poor teacher–student relationships. Gender altered the experience, but left both boys and girls with few useful school leaving qualifications.

Only two of the ten participants left school with the benchmark five or more good GCSE equivalents. Most left school without fulfilling their potential. At the heart of this lay teacher–student relationships that were fraught with difficulties and underpinned by negative racial stereotyping. Low teacher expectations affected the girls most and were characterized by streaming them into low-ability groups and providing poor careers advice. Several participants faced numerous obstacles and had to challenge their teachers' authority or ignore their advice in order to achieve. The absence of outright conflict with teachers does not deny the teachers' roles in hindering the girls' progress: four of the five left school with qualifications equivalent to only two or three good GCSEs.

Conflict with teachers affected the boys even more. They received much encouragement for sports, but teachers gave little encouragement for the students' academic endeavours. The boys' masculine identities seemed to accentuate the difficulties they experienced in school and several expressed having lacked interest and motivation to learn. Four of the five boys left school without good GCSE equivalents.

To survive in a system that disparaged them, the girls persisted in their academic pursuits in the face of adversity. They fought the system from within and managed to achieve some academic success. The boys diverted their energies to the more rewarding endeavours of friendship groups and sports. Unlike the girls, they fought from outside the system and achieved success and status in non-academic pursuits.

Negative racial stereotyping is insidious, invidious and extremely difficult to challenge. The importance of improving diversity in schools via the proactive training of educators and the broadening of the curriculum cannot be over-emphasized. Increasing the presence of anti-racist and black teachers in schools would help to reduce the unfair treatment experienced by many black children and mitigate the soul-destroying impact of racism in its many forms within the system. In addition, African-Caribbean parents would benefit from greater involvement and awareness of how best to support their children in school. It should be incumbent upon schools to facilitate engagement of this kind by encouraging open dialogue and genuine collaboration.

# Notes

[1] O levels and CSEs preceded GCSEs as the standard school leaving qualifications. O level grades A to E are equivalent to GCSE grades A* to E. A grade 1 CSE (the highest grade attainable) is equivalent to a grade C O level or GCSE, making CSEs a lower-status qualification.

# Chapter 3

# En route to higher education: Motivations and journeys

They are driven by … 'educational urgency', a desire to succeed against the odds.

(Mirza, 2005: 9)

## Introduction

This chapter discusses the motivations and journeys of participants from the time they left compulsory schooling until their entry to higher education. To compensate for a lack of school leaving qualifications most spent extended periods in post-compulsory education (that is, sixth form or further education college). Just two of the ten interviewees followed the traditional route to university for their subject. For the others, the journey en route to higher education involved serendipity and stepping stones. Participants' experiences fell into two broad categories.

One cohort remained in education after compulsory schooling, intent on achieving qualifications for career progression. However, as a consequence of the low teacher expectations and poor careers advice that had affected their schooling, they spent longer than average in post-compulsory education, negotiating educational stepping stones.

The second cohort returned to education as adults. Their journeys involved serendipity and a specific catalyst. Most went through a range of transitions, embarking on employment, self-employment and various education and training courses before entering higher education.

The participants' motivations to enter higher education were primarily social mobility, pleasure of studying, family expectations and community activism. Financial hardship emerged as the main deterrent and was closely linked to the issue of time poverty. Their socio-economic status and their mature age ensured that many had to juggle work and family commitments.

The dynamics of race, ethnicity and social class influenced their choice of higher education institution, so most attended polytechnics or post-1992 universities. African-Caribbean social capital was a source of careers advice, academic advice and social networks that were key to their achievement.

## Serendipity and stepping stones on the path to higher education

There is an over-representation of African-Caribbean women in post-compulsory education, where their ambition and drive for qualifications enable them to overcome considerable difficulties relating to race, class and gender in pursuit of career success (Mirza, 2005). Similarly, there is an over-representation of black and minoritized students in higher education (ECU, 2014) and they tend to spend longer periods in adult education than their white peers pursuing professional and graduate qualifications (Modood and Acland, 1998). This was the case for most of my research group, who either remained in continuing education or took a short break before returning to adult education and achieving their degrees. Eight of the ten graduated in their twenties and two, having run their own businesses, returned to education later and graduated in their thirties.

Just two interviewees followed the traditional path to higher education for their degree courses. The other eight followed non-traditional routes involving a year out, resits, Access courses, Higher National Diplomas, full-time employment or running their own business. They made gradual progress towards the often hazy idea of a better career. About half set their sights on higher education while in compulsory schooling. For others, university was not an option during school and the decision to pursue higher education signalled a change in the direction of their life.

Knowles et al. (1998) examine andragogy, which is a particular mode of learning relating to adults. They posit that adults' readiness to learn is usually stimulated by a change in life circumstances that creates a 'need to know'. Consequently, the adult re-enters a formal learning environment in pursuit of new qualifications and skills. Several of my participants referred to a turning point in their lives when the need to know became a driving force. Their paths to higher education were serendipitous and an unplanned sequence of events spurred them on. This often involved a transition of some sort that resulted in their (re-)discovery of an aptitude for academic endeavours and an interest in a particular subject. They experienced a change of circumstances or received encouragement from somebody significant. The catalysts for Zac were a yearning for a more fulfilling career and observing his peers progress to university:

I did not want to do one of these Youth Training Programmes ...
I didn't like the school at all but I thought, 'What the heck, just
go ...' Just to please my mum ... I think I did about four O levels
and I really surprised myself that I actually got an O level. And I
thought that's it; that's as far as I'll go ... [Then] one of the friends
who I'd studied with got accepted on to an A level course at the
local college and so I thought, 'Yeah, that's the kind of course I
want to do as well. Let me just try' ... I did a few other O levels as
well, during that time. The A level was in Art and Design. Passed
that, surprisingly again and then I thought after that, 'That's as
far as I'll go...' I thought, 'OK look ... try to find myself a factory
job or something' ... I couldn't think beyond that ... I got a job
at [a local] factory, which I did not enjoy at all. That was almost a
turning point. That said to me, 'You know what, I'm not cut out for
factory work.' And then I got a job at the [local] Afro-Caribbean
Cultural Centre ... I was the Publicity Officer ... I enjoyed it ...
Then after a year there, I took a step back and thought, 'I can do
a bit more than this. I know there's something else for me out
there' ... Then I met up with a couple of old friends, who were
on these degree courses. I'm like, 'How can you be on a degree
course? I know you're just as daft as I am!' And I thought, 'If they
can do it, I can [and] it's got to be better than what I've got at the
moment.' So I got on to a Foundation Course; again surprised
myself. Got through that ... Then I actually got on to a degree
course ... There were a few friends I had at the time ... We're all
the same age, grew up together and everything, but they were two
years ahead of me in their course. And just through seeing them
and knowing them and seeing them get through it, that gave me
more encouragement to say that if they can do it, I can do it too.

(Zac, entrepreneur)

Sean, by contrast, went through a traumatic period of transition, in which
his business folded, his relationship broke down and he went through a kind
of metamorphosis that made higher education seem like a viable option:

My brother had just started an Access course ... and he bounced
lots of ideas off me ... that kind of inspired me ... I was doing
these [short] courses, because I wanted to get back into business
... and [my teacher] said, 'You should just really go for a degree
instead of doing all these bits and bobs of courses ...Get yourself

a profession and then ... get the resources to [start] up your own business again.'

(Sean, housing advice manager)

Neil also cited an encouraging teacher in post-compulsory education as the catalyst for his educational progress. He suggested that, in spite of high expectations from his family and church community and his own academic ambitions, he felt that he had stumbled along doing poorly in school and college, until he struck up a good relationship with a particularly positive college teacher:

[He] was a really good teacher and ... I [applied] to universities and polytechnics and he did the reference. I had such a good rapport with him ... and it got me into higher education and I think without that I wouldn't have done very well.

(Neil, IT trainer)

On leaving school with three O levels, Nora completed a secretarial course. She described her catalyst as a political awakening relating to her racial identity:

I worked for the Race Issues Officer and he really helped me to understand who I am as a black person and I worked for the Training and Development Officer who was an amazing man ... He was like, 'Nora, you're amazing, you're so fantastic. You shouldn't be a secretary. Go and study more. You should go to uni ...' and he started to put the idea of university into my head ... So he encouraged me to go and do A levels and he paid for the [course], paid for my books, gave me time off work, because he really believed in me and that was a turning point for me. So as well as feeling good about myself as a black person, [I] also felt good about myself as an [intelligent person] ... nobody had ever said that I was intelligent.

(Nora, headteacher)

For Eve, it was a gradual process and the realization that health issues might compel her to consider a career change from hairdressing:

[The minister] saw things in me that he thought could be developed in terms of going on and doing more studying in the church. But I didn't have any ambitions in Religious Studies or Theology work ... Then we had another minister [and] he was very, very good ... He was the one that actually first put it to me to go and study Theology [and my brother-in-law] was very instrumental in encouraging me to go on an Access course. He said 'Would you think about going to university?'

(Eve, entrepreneur/teacher)

These narratives suggest that the people who acted as catalysts and facilitated the redirection of these participants towards higher education fell into two categories. Some were peers who had studied in university and thus presented it as an achievable objective, such as Zac's friends, Sean's brother and Eve's brother-in-law. Others were people in positions of authority in the participants' lives who believed in their capabilities; these included Nora's manager, Eve's minister and both Sean's and Neil's college teachers. Such encouragement contrasted with their school experiences and that of many other African-Caribbean school children, according to the literature (e.g. Mac an Ghaill, 1988; Mirza, 1992), where a marked absence of role models and mentors to offer direction was more typical. My interviewees alluded to the fact that their peers were not achieving academically in school, that teachers neither recognized nor encouraged the development of their academic abilities and that their parents were ill equipped to guide and facilitate their academic success.

Knowles *et al.* (1998) recognize that often a key individual acts as a catalyst for a mature student. Channer (1995) identifies that successful African-Caribbean students often encounter a 'benevolent individual', who assists with careers or academic advice, compensating for the shortcomings in the system. The additional dynamic evident in my research was that in the vast majority of cases, these individuals were African-Caribbean and/or actively involved in improving conditions in African-Caribbean communities. They, therefore, represented one element of a uniquely African-Caribbean social capital.

Social capital here refers to a network of people who provide support, knowledge and encouragement that facilitate entry into higher education. Yosso (2005) addresses the ways that social capital enhances the educational prospects of minoritized students. When my participants talked about benevolent individuals, they usually mentioned the race of that key person or their connection to an African-Caribbean community without attaching significance to it. However, this was a recurring factor in my participants' journeys to higher education and then later, during their higher education.

In a racialized society such as the UK, a person's attitude to race can be instrumental in enabling them to transcend racial barriers and support minoritized learners. This is because we live in a system of racist signification, which means that people make assumptions about people based on their (perceived) race. The literature that deconstructs whiteness (e.g. Sewell, 1997) explores the reasons for this. Race is a social construct rather than a biological distinction (Singh, 2004). In other words, the significance we attach to race is learned through social interactions and is not supported by scientific evidence. Pearce (2005) traces the development of her own understanding of race as a white teacher in a multi-ethnic classroom. She notes that the privileged position of whiteness in a system of racist signification enables white people to believe that they are the norm and therefore have no racial identity. This makes it easier to adopt a colour-blind approach and avoid dealing with uncomfortable issues relating to race and racism. She suggests that for people who identify as white to deal effectively with diversity, they must raise their awareness of racism, reflect on their own and others' (mis)understandings about race and challenge racism consistently, as a matter of duty. Only then, she argues, can they effectively deal with racial inequality.

Minoritized people cannot easily adopt a colour-blind approach, because they are constructed as having racial identities (Dabydeen *et al.*, 2007) and occupy a disadvantaged position within the system of racist signification. The life experience of being 'othered' is likely to heighten their awareness of racial identities and the dynamics of racism. So the fact that most of the benevolent individuals my participants spoke about were black or immersed in black communities is significant.

Furthermore, the participants' close identification with the key person because of their race, ethnicity or ethnic understanding may have made them more receptive to the influence of that person. This emphasizes the importance of having black and anti-racist people in key positions, where they can encourage the achievement of African-Caribbean students.

Within a few years of leaving compulsory education, the career aspirations of most of my interviewees crystallized their need for better qualifications. In many cases, the encouragement of peers, teachers or managers kindled their desire to achieve academically and affirmed their ability to do so.

## Motivations to study in higher education

The motivations for further study concentrated around social mobility, the pleasure of studying and family expectations. The dynamic of community activism also emerged. Many of the factors that motivate entry into higher education are universal, but the emphasis can vary considerably in relation to race, class, gender and age. Reay (2003) found that the motivations for working-class women to return to education as mature students were more likely to be intrinsic factors, such as an interest in the subject, than they were for younger students, whose motives were more instrumental and goal oriented. She highlighted a community orientation, which contrasts with the individualistic motives that are more characteristic of middle-class students. Men are inclined to undergo work-related education and training, whereas women undertake a much wider variety of courses, the desire to learn being central (McGivney, 2004). Alison Allen (1998) demonstrated that teachers and friends were more influential for white students, while family expectations were more important to minoritized students. For minoritized students the acquisition of qualifications was a pragmatic means to economic and career success in the face of their disadvantaged position in the employment market. These sentiments are largely echoed among my cohort.

Only two of my interviewees had a graduate parent with first-hand experience of the British education system, but most had internalized strong family discourses about education being a passport to success. The benefits of education were seen to be self-improvement and confidence-building.

Knowles *et al.* (1998) assert that internal motivators, such as quality of life, satisfaction and self-esteem, are most important to adult learners, but that personal drives and instrumentality go hand in hand. Sean confirmed this when he said:

> When I went to university I really wanted to progress and the drive was within me ... It was my discipline and my self-determination and I really wanted to do it ... I didn't want to do it to prove anything to anyone else.
>
> (Sean, housing advice manager)

Widening life choices, increasing earning potential and improving career prospects were the principal motivators for my interviewees, and these factors promote social mobility. Rather than aspiring to a typical British middle-class habitus, they stressed the practical benefits of career progression as the way to a more comfortable lifestyle.

When discussing social mobility some participants described their desire to avoid the poverty trap in which their parents found themselves. Michelle was crystal clear:

> I think escaping from my family background ... I just remember us being very poor and not having things ... I had my first job when I was 15, because I was just determined to have some

money … and I knew from quite early on that I needed to get out of that house if I didn't want to be like this. And if I stayed there and didn't go to university or do something different, then I was going to end up like this.

(Michelle, teacher)

Similarly, Neil explained:

My parents were a major [motivation], because they came over here and obviously they had no qualifications. My mother was a dressmaker at home … and my father started off working in a factory and retired as a bus driver. And he did so many hours and all that for a pittance. And I thought, 'That's not going to happen to me.' And it was not their fault, because they came over to this country and it's the way it is. But, you know, me being born here, education's given to us and I thought, 'Just take advantage.' So, I always thought I should do well.

(Neil, IT trainer)

The desire to improve career prospects was not necessarily part of a specific career strategy. Rather, the participants embarked on studying in higher education with a general sense that it would lead to better prospects:

I just thought [studying Hispanics] would be interesting. I never thought about it in terms of what would I be at the end of it … you assume that going to university would be a better thing to do than not going.

(Elaine, consultant)

Elaine assumed that university would lead to better opportunities, and Zac and others said much the same, referring to enjoying their subjects because of the 'interest' and 'comfort' they brought:

From what I knew the YTS [Youth Training Scheme][1] was like bricklaying, outdoor work, nothing at all of interest to me … Financially, obviously I'm kind of thinking I've got to [earn a living] and I've got to do something else I'm comfortable with. The creative side of things was definitely it. And as a kid I was always making things and Industrial Design Engineering, which I knew nothing about three years before I was on the course, was absolutely spot on for me. That's what I thought just before I applied for it.

(Zac, entrepreneur)

Alison Allen (1998) found that factors linked to the pleasure of studying, such as delaying employment, enjoying student life and personal development, motivate white students more than they do minoritized students. My findings show that delaying employment was unimportant to the interviewees but that the pleasure of studying was a very popular motivation. This exposes an oversight in the literature that explores black experiences of higher education.

Hughes *et al.* (2007) observe that the relationship between pleasure and learning has received little attention to date, largely because the literature on higher education currently emphasizes utilitarianism. They warn that an over-emphasis on the extrinsic rewards of education, such as improved earning potential, can lead to an increasingly market-driven approach that focuses on measurable outcomes at the cost of intellectual enquiry.

The narratives of some participants did suggest that university was an end in itself and embarked upon for intrinsic satisfaction and a sense of achievement. Michelle explained her enjoyment and sense of belonging in a learning environment:

> For me just getting to university and getting a degree – that was my aim ... I loved [being in a learning environment]. I loved it. I think it's the place where I always feel myself; the most at ease, the most productive.
>
> (Michelle, teacher)

Respondents evoked the word 'love' as they recaptured the feelings that drove their desire to study. Nora, for instance, spoke of her love of the subject:

> Once I did my A level in Psychology, which is the first A level I did, I thought, 'I love this subject.' I thought, 'Wow, there's nothing better than this.'
>
> (Nora, headteacher)

And Eve enthused about the light-bulb moment that illuminated her love of the subject and love of learning:

> It was actually a Sociology class to do with the church and society and I remember just sitting in and I thought how fantastic it was ... I'd found my little niche ... And I thought, 'Gosh this is really good.' I absolutely loved it ... It was the subject that I loved more than anything else. That's what gave me the motivation ... I have been a bit of a sponge with my studying and maybe that's why

I did well at uni; because I just loved learning and finding more out about things.

(Eve, entrepreneur/teacher)

Leroy provided a heartfelt description of the satisfaction he derived from his subject and the hopes and dreams, which fuelled his desire to study. He conveyed a sense of loss and a yearning to return to the lifestyle in which he immersed himself in the pure pleasure of learning his subject:

Terence Conran ... He created Habitat. That's who I pictured myself as. But, it was a sort of a glazy dream. In the 1950s they would have photographs taken of him on his designer chair or something. It was a bit like the equivalent of the 'Rebel Without a Cause', James Dean sitting on his bike ... Now that's what I envisaged for myself [laughs]. I mean I pictured myself as successful as him, not a designer working with loads of other designers in an office. But as I started to get a grip on reality, I realized that design isn't just a single-person process ... All these French and London designers, that's how I pictured myself ... And it was sort of religious for me to go to central London every week to either an exhibition, a design gallery or visit the Design Council to pick up a book on design. That was my life. I couldn't think of not doing that. And now I rarely do that. I'd like to get back into it. And I used to sit on trains or buses and sketch people. That's what I used to do. I was a bit of a bohemian.

(Leroy, further education (FE) lecturer)

Hughes *et al.* (2007) provide a refreshing exploration of the relationship between pleasure and learning. They explain that discourses about motivation tend to view the student as a mind, whereas discussions about desires tend to view the student as a physical body. 'Embodied pedagogy' aims for a synthesis of the two. However, as human beings we are comprised of not only mind and body but also soul. Pleasure, it seems, is one way that the soul manifests itself, directing us on our journey through life by creating desires or longings within us. Their use of emotive language, such as 'love' and 'I couldn't think of not doing that', suggests that the forces propelling and sustaining participants' higher education study went beyond the logic of the mind and the urges of the body, to the deeply felt realms of the soul.

Drawing on Jung, psychology and theology, Moore (1992) highlights the difficulty of providing a clear definition of the soul. For the purpose of this book, I interpret the soul as the place deep within us from which strong emotions, inner drives and motivations emerge. The soul is the spirit and life force of a human being that resides within the outer shell of the physical body and is closely associated with matters of the heart. In Moore's words:

> Tradition teaches that soul lies midway between understanding and unconsciousness, and its instrument is neither the mind nor the body ... Fulfilling work, rewarding relationships, personal power, and relief from symptoms are all gifts of the soul.
>
> (Moore, 1992: xi)

When Moore (1992) discusses power, he distinguishes between the way it operates in the ego and will, and the way power operates within the soul. He states:

> When we want to accomplish something egoistically, we gather our strength, develop a strategy, and apply every effort ... using brute strength and narrow, rationalistic vision. The power of the soul, in contrast, is more like a great reservoir or, in traditional imagery, like the force of water in a fast-rushing river. It is natural, not manipulated, and stems from an unknown source.
>
> (Moore, 1992: 119)

I see clear parallels between the energy of Moore's (1992) soul power and the role of pleasure as a stimulus for my participants' learning. Leroy unwittingly made an analogy with spirituality when he said: 'it was sort of religious for me'. The satisfaction these participants derived from learning unleashed a deep-rooted desire to learn more and more. The strength of feeling was such that continuing to learn became the natural process and *not* continuing with their education became unthinkable.

When hooks (1994) explores the place of emotions in the classroom, she identifies that despite a common perception that 'to be truly intellectual we must be cut off from our emotions' (p. 115), we should, in fact, welcome the body and soul into the classroom. My findings concur, suggesting that engaging the students' soul, along with mind and body, can indeed enrich the learning process.

There was a marked difference in how the men and women interviewed spoke about their pleasure in studying. The literature emphasizes the pragmatic reasons for education given by minoritized students (e.g. job opportunities) and seldom explores gender differentials. Yet, in their questionnaire responses all five of my female interviewees, but none of the men, cited pleasure as a *major* motivation. Similarly, four of the five participants who spoke about their love of learning or subject were women.

While the extrinsic rewards of education mattered to all respondents, the additional gender dynamic suggests that pleasure was a very important contributory factor, particularly for the women, in their pursuit of higher education.

As the literature suggests (e.g. Rhamie, 2007), family expectation was important in motivating my interviewees to embark on continuing education. Encouragement from their families propelled them into adult education, but they were generally not expected to progress to higher education. Most of the female participants perceived their family's expectation as support and encouragement for their own decision to study. The male participants, however, were more inclined to experience family expectations as a pressure, especially when older siblings had achieved highly:

> When I reached 16 ... my mum thought I was really clever ... and expected me to stop on at school to do my O levels ... I didn't actually get any O levels or CSEs when I left ... [She] thought I could do a lot more ... It was not that I wanted to stay, [but] because she expected me to stay.
>
> (Zac, entrepreneur)

Zac left compulsory schooling with no qualifications and his school refused him a place in their sixth form. Despite this and his lack of enthusiasm about remaining in school, Zac's mother's high expectations and continuing belief in his ability led him to apply to a neighbouring school's sixth form, where he was admitted.

Similarly, Dean left school without qualifications, but his mother's expectations ultimately led him to university:

> My mum ... was very adamant that you need to go through the education system in order to get something ... As a younger child I had a lot of pressure on me to achieve, because my sisters were achievers and were 'A' students ... They expected me to be just like my sisters and I always felt that it was expected of me to achieve.
>
> (Dean, youth worker)

The pressure to keep up with siblings described by Dean was echoed by Neil's narrative:

> [My parents] encouraged me a lot ... They always made sure we did homework. My brother definitely had homework, because he went to grammar school ... I went to a comprehensive and they gave us things, but nothing like the grammar school would and

so I tried to make my own homework, just to please my parents ... and it's always been, '[Your brother's] good at this, [your brother's] doing that,' and then when he passes nine O levels, everyone was saying ... 'Will you try to get ten to beat him?' and I couldn't even tell them that I was only doing four at the time. [Laughs] For me I've always thought it was quite difficult growing up in some respects, because I always had my brother to compete with ... I think my brother wanted to be a doctor ... and it wasn't until I finished university and I started teaching, which I was really comfortable in, when I actually stopped worrying about being compared to him.

(Neil, IT trainer)

Dean's and Neil's school experience did not correspond to their parents' high academic expectations of them and neither did their own perceptions of their ability. The boys did not see themselves as academic achievers and therefore felt pressured by their parents. But their parents' unwavering belief in them pushed and then sustained them on their educational paths. The fact that they started school as academic achievers, and later became graduates, indicates that they had latent ability, but perhaps lacked the self-belief or motivation to harness it. We saw in the previous chapter that peer pressure and negative racial stereotyping strongly affected boys. This combined with the parental pressure to achieve academically must have been very difficult to cope with.

Osborne (2001) describes 'academic disidentification' as the process that occurs when black boys imbibe the negative racial stereotypes and begin to detach their self-esteem from academic achievement. They instead identify with characteristics such as sporting prowess, which conform to the stereotypical images of black masculinities. Most of the male participants in my research recognized their own athletic ability and were encouraged to develop it at school, but this was not the case with their academic ability. The male experience of feeling pressured by parental expectations, in contrast to the female experience of feeling encouraged, may well have been a by-product of the boys' academic disidentification and the conflicting values emanating from the divergent social settings of home and school.

This is not only an issue of race but also of class. Jackson (2002) examines the links between 'laddishness' and the protection of self-worth, and Reay (2002) demonstrates how working-class masculinities can create a conflict for working-class boys. In 'Shaun's story', Reay (2002) uses Bourdieu's 'duality of self' to delve deeply into the contradictions experienced by a working-class boy striving for educational achievement while at the same time trying to maintain respect from his peers and a sense of belonging. She describes Shaun's juggling act of maintaining his local reputation for being 'tough' with working hard in class as requiring 'almost superhuman efforts' (Reay, 2002: 226), because 'he has to constantly guard against being reclassified as "a geek"' (Reay, 2002: 227). Drawing on Butler (1990, 1993), Archer and Francis (2007) suggest that gender is 'performed' and that different performances of gender carry different status. Being categorized as a 'geek' would reduce Shaun's status in terms of working-class masculinities. Whereas middle-class boys can belong to their peer group and succeed academically, this is not the case for working-class boys.

When my participants discussed family expectations they often went beyond the nuclear family and included community members as an extension of family. Often this community was the church, which also emerged as a theme in Channer's (1995) and Rhamie and Hallam's (2002) research into African-Caribbean academic achievers. These researchers note that a positive involvement in a supportive community, often the church, encourages African-Caribbean achievers. It also provides a protective barrier against the damaging effects of the negative images of black people that prevail in the UK's popular media. Michelle, Alison and Eve all spoke of their immersion in black churches, where black academic achievement was not only encouraged but also a norm. As Michelle said:

> I remember going to church and my friends were either at university already or going there and that was positive, because they would give you their experiences of being at university. The church I went to was African and Caribbean; mostly Caribbean.
>
> (Michelle, teacher)

The influence of the church on Eve directly motivated her to make the journey to higher education as an adult returner. The ministers strongly encouraged her and she ascribed the sense of belonging and the achievement orientation of the church as contributing to her academic achievement. Channer (1995) describes religion as 'a source of strength in [the] quest for academic success' (Channer, 1995: 111). She suggests that church communities provide a black support network that encourages academic development and helps in the fight against the dehumanization that is racism. Channer articulates that 'for many black people ... religion and education can be viewed as channels for freedom. Both provide a psychological and social framework within which black people can operate effectively in a racist society' (Channer, 1995: 190).

Among my participants, Alison was rather more sceptical regarding the role of the church. She felt that she benefitted from its encouragement to excel academically, but questioned the church's apparent passive acceptance of oppression and dominance. She pointed to the absence of political awareness in her church:

> There was a lack of self-history, whether that be African or Caribbean and a continual focus on a white God ... and the black people didn't complain about it. So, what's the real education?
>
> (Alison, HE lecturer)

Alison's critical comments reflect Freire's (1996) and hooks's (1994) belief that education should be a conduit for the liberation of the oppressed masses and that 'awakening critical consciousness' (Bravette, 1996: 3) should be the ultimate objective. Although Alison's church encouraged her academic endeavours, she developed her critical consciousness outside it.

Elaine's case was different. Her expectations to achieve came not from the church, but from her family's involvement in a black activist community. Political awareness was married to an emphasis on educational attainment and her participation in activities such as a supplementary Saturday school exposed her to black achievers, while also raising her awareness of positive elements of African heritage cultures. She explained:

> Maybe it is just like nurturing different parts of you in different ways ... I think it was important, because ... the vision you would have of black people might have been a lot more negative from what's fed through the media, really ... as an outcome of being exposed to things like ALD [Afrikan Liberation Day] and Saturday school ... you realize that there are things you take for granted that other people [don't know].
>
> (Elaine, consultant)

Elaine was unique among my interviewees in that her parents, school teachers and community all had high expectations of her. She also placed emphasis on political consciousness and was one of two interviewees to pursue a traditional route to higher education.

Political awareness and community activism emerged as additional motivating factors for the interviewees. This resonates to some extent with Reay's (2003) findings that commitment to community is a driving force for mature, working-class women who return to education. For my research participants, political awareness tended to revolve around issues relating to race and ethnicity and a desire to improve the living conditions of African-

Caribbean people in the UK. Nora talked about her political awakening and described the process of 'conscientization' (Freire, 1996) that stimulated her love of learning and drive to achieve:

Nora:  It wasn't until I started to work for the Race Issues Officer and he started to teach me [and] pointed me in the direction of books that I should be reading. We started up a group [and] I got some of my friends involved and we started to talk about black issues and that's when I really started to understand what it meant to be a black person. I mean growing up [during] primary school, I know I wanted to be white and I went through all of the people calling me names and wearing things on my head to try and get to have long hair ... But it was when I was like 18 [years old] and worked for the Race Issues Officer and he used to do a lot of the Race Equality Training and I really started to open my eyes about ... this is who I am ... this is the greatness of black people. I read a bit around Egyptology and about Africa and about all the things that black people have contributed. Slavery and all of that, which, I mean I got some of that from watching 'Roots'[2] and my mom ... helped to ground me in my ethnicity.

Amanda:  Do you think your black consciousness actually motivated you to go to university more or do you think it was just incidental?

Nora:  No, I think it motivated me, because I think I understood at that point that black people were capable of great things, where before I didn't really see that. I don't think there really were any role models for me to say, 'OK, well, they've been through university, you can do it, can't you?' and so I think it was when I was finding out all the fantastic things that black people had done and continued to do. I think that was an additional motivator for me ... say, 'Well yeah, you know, I'm capable of this, black people do do this.'

Dean discussed community activism as a motivating factor for him to follow the path into higher education and as something that helped him sustain his studies when he felt demotivated:

My motivation was a better job, having a say in the community and being able to talk on behalf of young people ... to represent

51

some people that aren't … and to be some kind of role model to both service users and other colleagues … I wanted to contribute to a voice in the community … the black community, especially young males, to kind of explain that we need to find different ways of working to our white counterparts. You need to find different ways of working, because there's a missing link here.

(Dean, youth worker)

Nora and Dean explicitly cited commitment to community development as a motivating factor to study. The connection between education and the politics of race was also evident in the narratives of Alison and Elaine. Most participants expressed a desire to enhance the opportunities of future generations of African-Caribbean people in Britain, which indicates their conscientization and growing understanding of how the structures of society shape our lives and how they, as individuals, could use their agency to reshape this.

## Financial constraints and time poverty as the main deterrents

The most obvious barrier to higher education for most participants was their negative school experience. However, once they were intent on higher education, financial constraints became the most prominent hindrance.

Since the late 1990s government education policy has declared an agenda of widening participation and social inclusion to open up opportunities for adult education to a wider cross-section of society. Both Kennedy (1997) and Dearing (1997) identified funding mechanisms as the most appropriate way to encourage inclusion and challenge one of the principal barriers to continuing and adult education: poverty. However, decades of government policies that have eroded support, and the increasing costs of higher education, have largely negated these initiatives. Phasing out maintenance grants and housing benefits, alongside introducing ever-increasing tuition fees and repayable student loans, leaves poorer students with the additional burden of large debts at the end of their studies. This, combined with the lower return on investment experienced by minoritized people (TUC, 2016), mature students, working-class students and women (Reay, 2003), has resulted in discouraging outcomes for more and more people attending university.

Consequently, the cost of studying was the greatest deterrent for my respondents. The financial difficulties of studying in post-compulsory education are an issue of social class. Sean, who became a mature student in his thirties, described the dilemma he faced in relation to the financial cost of studying:

> The financial considerations really made me think that maybe I wasn't going to do it … I'd done the Business Studies course, the Computing course and then I was enrolling on the Access course and it took me probably a year, year and a half before I did anything, because I was so disillusioned … So, during this time I'd not been in full-time employment and then I had to … say, 'Well, you've got another three years before you can actually go back [to] full-time employment.' … So that was a real deterrent in terms of lack of earning power if you are doing full-time studies.
>
> (Sean, housing advice manager)

His initial reservations were borne out by the debts he accumulated and compounded by the demands of working while studying:

> Well, I got a grant for the course and I got a partial grant for survival, but that didn't pay the rent as well as living expenses. So I had to go to do part-time work in [a local factory]. So I'd zoom and go straight to [work] and do 5 p.m. till 9 p.m. … That was one of the biggest strains I had … I went into debt [with] my rent … I went to court for it; got suspended possession orders for it. That was hanging over me while I was doing the course, which doesn't help, because it was stressful in terms of workload, because a lot of the time I had to work … in terms of the bills that were building up, because I still had to pay my water rates and everything else.
>
> (Sean, housing advice manager)

Even those with marketable skills were not immune to the financial problems caused by studying:

> Other barriers … financial. It's a strain going to university. I worked. I was lucky. Because I was a secretary, I could type. Every Christmas, Easter and summer holiday I typed my fingers off, so that I could sustain my university life … They gave you grants then and I was lucky, because I could get a grant [because] we were on Income Support [social security benefit]. So that was a big barrier, because I was working and I had to give up the job – no money. But because I could type I managed to earn … It could have seriously deterred me. And that's why in my final

year I lived with my aunt, because I was getting into debt, so I needed to be rent free. [Laughs] So having the family there was very good for me.

(Nora, headteacher)

Financial difficulties were accentuated for the mature students who returned to education after a period of employment. Although they appreciated being able to earn, they performed a fine balancing act that required strict discipline:

Financial difficulties come in [and] going from full-time work I had to really plan. I didn't know if I could afford to go to university or to even stop working full time to do the Access course. So I [worked] out that if I worked two full days or two and a half that would be OK ... It was hard going ... All the way through I've not stopped working.

(Eve, entrepreneur/teacher)

One of the consequences of financial constraint was the knock-on effect of time poverty, particularly for those struggling to balance studies with work and family commitments. Reay (2003) points out that the mature working-class women in her research were forced to juggle their work with their family responsibilities. Time poverty was a serious hindrance and motherhood compounded this considerably. Women usually perform the role of primary carer for children (Hughes, 2002), so the difficulties faced by mature students are often greater for women students. Time poverty emerged as an issue for both the women and men in my research and it is significant that none had primary responsibility for childcare during their undergraduate studies. This may well have been a key factor in their ability to complete.

Solórzano (1998) notes that 'strength', 'determination' and 'persistence' are essential for 'scholars of color' to survive in the academy. These characteristics were evident among my interviewees in their struggle to balance their commitments. Many had to manage their studies alongside the competing demands of working full or part time, numerous courses and intensive study routes.

A prime example of this was Eve, who while running a business, simultaneously studied for a Lay Preachers Training course by distance learning alongside an Access course and then a degree course. She attained a first class honours degree, but described the struggle to finish her Lay Preachers course as a real test of her perseverance in the face of extreme tiredness. Similarly, Nora described her single-mindedness, when a few years after leaving school, she achieved three A grades at A-level to obtain entry into a prestigious university:

> I was determined. I got up at 5 o'clock in the morning and studied before I went to work. And then when everybody had left work I would stay at work and study. I was like, tunnel vision. Friends were like, history. I didn't use to see anybody, because I knew I was going to university ... It was the hardest thing. I was just work, study, work, study and that was it ... and that was determination ... my personal motivation from university through to MA has helped me more than any other influence.
>
> (Nora, headteacher)

Reay (2003) notes that adult returners often sacrifice care of the self in the pursuit of qualifications and find themselves exhausted and unable to maintain their existing friendships. For my participants, self-motivation and focus emerged as central to transcending their difficulties. A larger than average proportion of minoritized and working-class students drop out of university (hooks, 1994; Modood and Acland, 1998; ECU, 2014). Dean had been determined to resist that fate:

> I left university about 15 times. I said, 'I'm not coming back. I don't like it.' And that was due to me putting myself under pressure, because I had three jobs when I went to university.
>
> (Dean, youth worker)

The drive and determination of my respondents illustrate the tenacity that enabled them to achieve in the face of considerable difficulty.

## Race and class dynamics in choice of higher education institution

Minoritized students tend to be concentrated in 'new' universities and in London (Ball *et al.*, 2002). There is no consensus over the factors that determine their choice, but there is evidence of an inclination to study close to home and a preference for institutions with an ethnically diverse population (Taylor, 1992; Allen, A., 1998). Ball *et al.* (2002) addressed the impact of social class and ethnicity on university choices and found that class was the dominant factor. Their research population included a large Jewish cohort – an invisible minority – which might, arguably, obscure the issue of race. Additionally, Reay (2003) found that mature working-class students were attracted to post-1992 universities as they felt more comfortable and welcome there.

**Table 3.1:** Undergraduate study

| Name | Qualification | University type |
|------|---------------|-----------------|
| Nora | BA (Hons) Psychology | Old |
| Elaine | BA (Hons) Hispanic Studies | Old |
| Michelle | BSc (Hons) Export Engineering | New |
| Alison | BA (Hons) Combined Arts (Linguistics and Psychology) | New |
| Eve | BA (Hons) Religious Studies | New |
| Neil | HND Computer Technology and Cert Ed in FE | New |
| Sean | BA (Hons) Sociology | Old |
| Dean | BA (Hons) Combined Community and Youth Studies | New |
| Zac | BA (Hons) Three Dimensional Design | New |
| Leroy | BA (Hons) Product and Furniture Design | New |

Issues of race, as well as class, influenced my interviewees' choice of higher education institution. About half were the first in their family or immediate social network to attend university. Subjects and grades were determinants in their choices of higher education institution, but the prospect of fitting in was a significant factor. Table 3.1 shows that the majority opted for 'new' universities.

They also selected higher education institutions that offered proximity to black social networks; some achieved this by remaining close to their family:

> I chose Nottingham as well, because I had [my cousins] down the road ... I went to my aunt every Sunday. I used to meet my mum there. That counted for a lot ... Birmingham was [also close] so I went home very often.
>
> (Nora, headteacher)

Others attended institutions that were ethnically diverse or in ethnically diverse locations. Zac's approach combined the two:

> [I chose] definitely based on a place that's got black people around; most definitely. If it didn't, it could have been one of the best places in the world, but I wasn't going to go there if I didn't

feel comfortable ... I didn't really move far away from home ...
I didn't really lose touch with my friends, 'cause they were still
quite close anyway.

(Zac, entrepreneur)

Nora was clear that race and class dynamics influenced her thinking. She described her attraction to the leafy campus at the prestigious university of her choice:

I think Nottingham looked like a place where scholars were ...
you know the old buildings, the history, you know. [Laughs] So
I quite liked that ... I quite fancied myself in that kind of place.

(Nora, headteacher)

But she had reservations about not fitting in on the grounds of both her race and class:

Going to university, one of the first things I did notice was the
lack of black people and ... I was a bit frightened. I was a bit,
'I don't know whether I wanna do this?' ... Me knowing that I
come from an area where nobody goes to university, I felt that,
would I have anything in common with even the black people?
Was I gonna have anything in common with anybody? ... So, it
wasn't just a black thing, it was a class thing as well.

(Nora, headteacher)

Ball *et al.* (2002) use Bourdieu's concept of social capital to explore the different ways minoritized people from working-class and middle-class backgrounds select higher education institutions. The theory suggests that social capital gives middle-class students a distinct advantage in selecting the 'best' higher education institutions to attend, as they can use their social connections to gain insight into which well-resourced and high-status universities maximize career prospects. Ball *et al.* (2002) subdivide their research subjects into two categories: 'contingent choosers' and 'embedded choosers'. The former tended to be the first generation in their families to attend university and working class; the latter tended to be members of middle-class families with a history of university attendance. So the 'embedded choosers' had access to middle-class social capital.

My participants were predominantly 'contingent choosers' so according to Ball *et al.* (2002) '[t]heir social capital is of limited relevance here' (p. 338). On the contrary, I suggest that most tapped into their own unique African-Caribbean social capital, which was different to middle-class social capital but not irrelevant. My interviewees used their black social networks to insulate themselves against the isolation they anticipated in higher education. Rhamie (2007) suggests that community networks help African-Caribbean academic achievers to be resilient and this is a protective barrier against their negative experiences in education. In my study, participants used the African-Caribbean social capital of community networks to create a protective barrier against social isolation and the 'outsider' feelings that contribute to high drop-out rates among minoritized and working-class students. They were thus able to achieve a workable balance between maintaining a rootedness in their African-Caribbean identity and ensuring success in higher education. This ultimately facilitated a degree of social mobility through educational attainment that may otherwise have been beyond their reach. (The role of black support networks in higher education is discussed in Chapter 4, which explores higher education experiences.)

Reay (2001) questions whether their quest for self-improvement results in working-class students finding or losing themselves when they move away from their existing identity that is embedded in working-class norms, into the middle-class arena of higher education. She observes:

> The working-class mature students were trying to negotiate a difficult balance between investing in a new improved identity and holding on to a cohesive self that retained an anchor in what had gone before.
>
> (Reay, 2001: 337)

Unlike Nora, others were guarded in their choice of higher education institution. Michelle explained her rationale for choosing a polytechnic for her undergraduate degree and only then feeling equipped to go to an elite university for postgraduate studies. She likened the differences between 'new' and 'old' universities to state and private schools and mentioned the stark difference between the limited resources at the polytechnic and those at the well-resourced university:

> I was more comfortable going to the polytechnic first ... I think I would have had an inferiority complex being among middle-class children who had been geared up for that sort of education, so by the time I got to Warwick University I was fine and I was amazed at the discrepancy between [the resources at] Birmingham Poly and Warwick University.
>
> (Michelle, teacher)

Michelle's comments also highlight the potential downside of selecting 'new' universities and her comments illustrate the way African-Caribbean learners can self-select out of certain educational opportunities. Reservations about fitting in can be a strong deterrent to attending 'old' universities, but choosing to avoid them can limit their future career prospects. Reay (2001) argues that government policy towards improving access for working-class students at the tertiary level of education has only failed them more by creating 'sink' universities. Reay (2003) suggests that 'old' universities could learn a great deal from 'new' universities in how to make non-traditional students welcome, if they truly wish to encourage social inclusion.

Michelle's comments above and Table 3.2 highlight another interesting dynamic that was apparent. After they had achieved their undergraduate degrees, most of the participants who progressed to postgraduate study elected to study at 'old' universities, completely reversing the undergraduate trend. Having succeeded in their studies at 'new' universities, they developed the desire and confidence to study at 'old' universities.

**Table 3.2:** Postgraduate study

| Name | Postgraduate qualification | University type |
| --- | --- | --- |
| Nora | PGCE: MA in Education Management | Old |
| Michelle | PGCE: MSc in IT for Manufacture | Old |
| Alison | MA in English Language Teaching | Old |
| Eve | MA in Religion and Public Life and PGCE | Old |
| Neil | PG Diploma in Management Studies MA in Human Resources PG Diploma in Project Management | New and old |
| Leroy | PGCE | New |

## Conclusions

In this chapter I explored the interviewees' pathways to higher education. The vast majority were non-traditional students and they progressed to higher education in a series of stepping stones, studying a range of courses and embarking on employment or self-employment. Approximately half had been intent on higher education during their schooling. For others, the route to higher education was serendipitous; being encouraged by one key person was often the catalyst. These key people represented an element of their unique African-Caribbean social capital, and illustrate why there needs to be black and anti-racist individuals in positions where they can positively encourage and promote African-Caribbean achievement.

Respondents were united in their belief that education was the key to success in life and that graduate career prospects would facilitate this. The most prominent motivation to study was social mobility, which corroborates the existing literature on race and higher education. Their families' high expectations of them was another key motivating factor, although this was experienced largely as encouragement by the female participants and as pressure by the males. My analysis of this gender difference is that black and working-class masculinities conspired to create low expectations from their school teachers, which conflicted with the high academic expectations of their parents. The women interviewed saw the pleasure of studying as being an important contributory factor. The love of learning that several of the women and one man described suggested that their desire to study for pleasure was connected to not only the mind and body but also the soul. Political awareness and community activism had also motivated them.

Once the participants had decided to study in higher education, financial constraints proved to be the main deterrent; social class was clearly an issue. Time poverty meant having to juggle work, study and family commitments. Determination was a strong characteristic that enabled them to transcend the many difficulties they encountered.

In addition to their subjects and grades, the interviewees were influenced by various race and class dynamics when selecting their higher education institution. Most pursued their undergraduate studies in post-1992 universities and tended to prefer institutions that were either ethnically diverse, close to family or in ethnically diverse areas. They tapped into African-Caribbean social capital in the form of social networks, which protected them from feeling isolated. For postgraduate studies the trend reversed and the vast majority attended old universities.

## Notes
[1] Youth Training Scheme – a government-sponsored training programme for young adults that operated from 1983 to 1989.
[2] Popular TV series (1977) that charted an African-American history by following Alex Haley's family tree from slavery to contemporary times.

# Chapter 4

# Learning to achieve: The higher education experience

Many professors have conveyed to me their feeling that the classroom should be a 'safe' place ... The experience of professors who educate for critical consciousness indicates that many students, especially students of color, may not feel at all 'safe' in what appears to be a neutral setting ... the politics of domination are often reproduced in the educational setting.

(hooks, 1994: 39)

## Introduction

In this chapter I explore the higher education experiences of my participants. Whereas their school experiences were largely about learning to fail, the emphasis in higher education was on learning to achieve. At this stage in their educational journeys, participants were better equipped to take control of their own learning and acquired valuable academic qualifications.

The literature on race and higher education rarely focuses on the specific experiences of African-Caribbean students. I examine how subtle racism is perpetuated through (a) a lack of diversity in staffing and curriculum and (b) microaggressions (Solórzano, 1998) in interactions between black students and academic staff. To survive and succeed, the participants used emotional withdrawal from certain teacher–student relationships, and benefitted from the encouragement and support of minoritized teaching staff. Some participants presented black perspectives in their coursework when possible, but recognized that this approach to the curriculum could be risky.

When I explore the experiences of participants through the lens of social class as non-traditional and mature students, three themes predominantly arise. Firstly, the feeling of not fitting in is a common experience. Secondly, the role of informal black support networks is an effective strategy to tackle isolation. Thirdly, respondents' insecurities about their own academic ability emerge as a key issue related to class and race.

To address the dearth of literature about the gendered experiences of African-Caribbean students in higher education, I explore the gender dynamic of postgraduate study among my participants. My findings reveal a strong inclination towards academia among the women, but a reluctance to embark on academic careers mainly due to social class barriers.

## Race in higher education

Interviewees identified the need for more black academic staff, a more multicultural core curriculum and more multicultural activities in higher education. Examining the experiences of students of African, Caribbean and Asian descent in British universities, Paul Allen (1998) found that the lack of diversity among higher education staff left black students vulnerable to racism from staff and unsupported by institutional structures. This, together with the lack of diversity in the curriculum, fuelled scepticism among minoritized students, who questioned why their cultures and histories were not validated in the institutional ethos, culture and curriculum.

Minoritized students tend to experience less supportive relationships with lecturers than their white peers (Allen, P., 1998) and many grapple with the low expectations lecturers hold of them (Reynolds, 2006). The gross under-representation of black academic staff (HESA, 2011) compounds this issue, indicating that race equality is not a priority for higher education institutions (Singh, 1998). Yet, many black students find black academic staff crucial role models and sources of support (Mukherjee, 2001), particularly when tackling subtle racism. This vital role is barely acknowledged by higher education institutions so the needs of black students frequently go unmet, while the few black academics addressing these needs face additional pressures (Channer and Franklin, 1995).

In British schools negative racial stereotyping by teachers lowers their expectations of black students and can cause conflict (Vincent *et al.*, 2011). My interviewees' narratives about school were littered with references to poor teacher–student relationships and the negative consequences for their performance. However, at university there was a marked difference in the way the participants managed their relationships with lecturers. Dean, for instance, felt that he had much better relationships with his teachers in university than in school, because of their flexible and personal approach, while Sean noted that his success at university was helped by not being dependent on good teacher–student relationships:

> [In school] there were some teachers which you got on with and
> so even though you may not have liked the subject you would

actually be productive in that class. But ... if you didn't get on with the teacher, if there was some sort of negative feedback from the teacher ... you'd do the bare minimum. And I found that all the way throughout my experience in the education system, apart from when I got to university and I found that I had total control over the learning process.

(Sean, housing advice manager)

The overall impression was that relationships with lecturers were generally distant and that emotional withdrawal was a survival strategy that averted antagonism. However, emotional withdrawal does nothing to ensure receiving sufficient support. Eve observed that the support offered to black and white students on her course was unequal. She recounted how requests by black students for support were ignored while extensive assistance was offered to white students in a similar position:

[Two black students had] difficulties, but I felt that [the lecturers] were being quite racist, because there were other white students who were struggling and they were seeing them. And one of the [white] girls who was struggling ... told me a lot of things about how she used to get really low grades and how the teachers had been helping her and they were really good ... And of course that wasn't happening with the [two black students], even though they were asking for help. But I'm pleased that the [black] guy got the help in the end, because he decided not to go through the teachers. He just went to the Support Services at the university, which was good. I think if [the black] lady had, it would have been better for her. She just had too much pride.

(Eve, entrepreneur/teacher)

At the other end of the achievement spectrum, Eve attained a first class honours degree and reflected on the lack of encouragement she received in comparison to her white counterparts with similarly high grades. She suspected that lecturers' low expectations of black students was the root cause of their reluctance to acknowledge her ability:

Right from the first year the teachers were already predicting who was going to get a first class ... [My classmate] said to me, 'The lecturers are saying to me that three people are going to get firsts and that's me and Jeff and you.' I said, 'Me!' She said, 'Oh, haven't they said that to you?' And I realized that they were saying [that] to the other two people, who were white, but they never, ever once said [it] to me ... until the third year ... I never got that encouragement at all ... But it was quite clear that they gave a lot of encouragement to the white students ... So it's almost like when they can see that you have the ability and you're proving their stereotypes wrong ... I don't know maybe they're expecting us black people to drop out. I don't know what their expectations were, but I don't think it was very high ... So it was almost like a shock [to them].

(Eve, entrepreneur/teacher)

Solórzano (1998) uses critical race theory to analyse the ways in which racism manifests itself in higher education. He identifies subtle, offensive put-downs as one main form of racism and sexism experienced by black scholars. These often unintentional microaggressions occur in numerous interactions within the institution and lecturers convey low expectations and racist attitudes. Some of my interviewees described unsatisfactory relationships with lecturers, in which they saw racism as an underlying element. Zac described a particularly difficult relationship:

This one teacher, she just couldn't stand me for some reason. I [thought], 'What is your problem?' And I don't go through life thinking, 'It's because I'm black,' and I don't want to get anything more because I'm black. I want to get there because I'm supposed to be there ... I've worked to be there. But she was just always knocking me and marking me down. It was like she just wanted me off the course.

(Zac, entrepreneur)

Although my participants observed injustices in the ways they and their black peers were treated, they accepted this as inevitable and perceived that overtly challenging the staff would be futile. Arguably, life in Britain ensures that minoritized people develop an acute awareness of various forms of racism, which equips them to differentiate between racism and other causes of friction. Subtlety is an inherent characteristic of microaggressions and it is one reason that covert racism is seldom investigated. It is all too easy for microaggressions to be dismissed as harmless misunderstandings that have been misinterpreted by a hypersensitive person. Zac understood the insidiousness of racism when he said: 'I don't go through life thinking, "It's because I'm black"'.

Solórzano (1998) encourages minoritized students to challenge every microaggression so that, by naming and investigating them, racism can be confronted in higher education institutions. Nonetheless, raising complaints can be counterproductive and the absence of effective support mechanisms to tackle covert racism leaves its victims vulnerable to the power dynamics of teacher–student relationships. So the students continue to suffer in silence. My participants' narratives suggest that, rather than expending the enormous amounts of energy required to fight these hostilities, students adopted coping strategies, distancing themselves from the academic staff in question. Zac explained his conscious decision not to be drawn into a confrontation with his lecturer:

> She done something one time [that] really, really riled me up, and I [thought], 'You know what, she wants me riled up, 'cause she wants me to fail ... so I'm just gonna take this shit and I want to finish this thing, 'cause I know what I'm good at and I'm good at this and you ain't ever gonna stop me from doing it. I don't care what they say.
>
> (Zac, entrepreneur)

Eve, when she finally received encouragement, distrusted her lecturer's motives:

> [The lecturer] in the third year ... started telling me that I could get a first ... But she was the only tutor then that had said that. Like she'd been saying to the other girl from the first year. But I was wary of her by then anyway, very wary. And it was in my mind, 'Why didn't you say that [before] and why didn't I get the same encouragement like the others?'
>
> (Eve, entrepreneur/teacher)

Black children who are successful in schools attach little importance to their teachers' assessments of their ability (Mac an Ghaill, 1988), developing resilience or a protective barrier (Rhamie and Hallam, 2002). According to Mirza (1992), African-Caribbean girls resist negativity from teachers by striving to exceed the teachers' low expectations. My participants' narratives indicate that black students employ similar survival strategies in higher education. For example, Eve noted that her black classmates' requests for help were ignored by lecturers. The male student bypassed the lecturers by tapping into other university support services, but the female student 'had too much pride' to seek assistance elsewhere and appeared to withdraw her expectations of support. Eve's comments below betrayed her own withdrawal of expectations and show how rebuffs from lecturers can cause black students to shun close relationships with them and to internalize a belief that expecting their support is a waste of time:

> It was quite clear that they gave a lot of encouragement to the white students, because you saw little things like some of the girls having coffee with them and all pally pally [very friendly] and that kind of stuff. But I was always happy to keep away from that, because I thought, 'I'm here to study and I don't need any pals basically from any of the lecturers.' I'd rather keep them there and I'm here. So that's the way I always played it.
>
> (Eve, entrepreneur/teacher)

Reynolds (2006) indicates that her respondents were sensitive to negative feedback from lecturers so were reluctant to seek further advice. Rodgers (2006) also suggests that black male students in his research were reluctant to use official university support services, seeing it as a mark of failure. While my research corroborates the evidence of both Reynolds (2006) and Rodgers (2006), it also identifies these behaviours as symptomatic of emotional withdrawal. This defence mechanism is developed as a shrewd response to the onslaught of the microaggressions and unfavourable treatment they encounter. Like uninvited guests or 'outsiders within' (Collins, 2000), they learn to maintain a distance from academic staff and have little expectation of support, becoming increasingly self-reliant.

The independent learning styles in higher education make it possible for students to distance themselves from teaching staff in a way that is not feasible in school. The disadvantages of such emotional withdrawal are played out in higher than average drop-out rates among minoritized students and lower than average degree classifications (ECU, 2014). Their silence about the racism they experience is not without cost. Bravette (1996) discusses the impact of her own silence over racism in the workplace:

> Though it may be politically expedient to remain silent, the personal cost is high in terms of the self-denial which is involved ... [people can] fall, inadvertently, into the trap of perpetuating the status quo through their silence and seeking of acceptance.
>
> (Bravette, 1996: 8)

The strategic use of emotional withdrawal reduced the potential for poor teacher–student relationships to have a negative impact. At the same time it enabled respondents to achieve academically in higher education, which contrasted markedly with their school experiences.

The presence of minoritized staff in teaching roles appeared to enhance the experiences of some students. Every one of my interviewees agreed that increasing the presence of black staff at various levels within higher education institutions would enhance the university experience. Channer (1995) found that successful African-Caribbean students had often encountered a 'benevolent individual' who assisted them in navigating the British education system. We have seen how the benevolent individuals who encouraged my interviewees en route to higher education were usually from minoritized backgrounds or immersed in minoritized communities. Their insight into black experiences enabled them to transcend the barriers of race and negative racial stereotyping. Similarly, in the rare instances that participants recollected a particularly supportive relationship with a member of teaching staff in university, the latter was invariably Asian or African-Caribbean. For example, Eve received a few words of comfort and concern from a Sikh lecturer during difficult times, which contrasted with the lack of encouragement from other academic staff throughout most of her degree course. A Sri Lankan teacher/technician supported Zac by opening his eyes to the potential of computer technology in his design work:

> There was one guy ... he was very good for me ... if it wasn't for him I wouldn't be doing what I'm doing now ... He turned into the Head of Computer Aided Design [CAD], but he was a technician at first, just helping people with all the CAD work ... up until that point I had no interest in computers whatsoever, and I work on computers now – that's my life ... He actually spent time with me and Dan. We were the only two black people [and] actually the only two in the whole year who took any interest in CAD ... I would say it was more of a friendship. He didn't force [it] ... It was just the way he came across. He made things seem a lot simpler than you thought it was and help was always there. So really, he was a major turning point ... He was a big influence ... big time.
>
> (Zac, entrepreneur)

Sean was motivated and encouraged by his black male tutor:

> [My tutor] happened to be a black guy. He was excellent... He just gave you that drive [and] extra encouragement saying, 'Come on, I know you can do it.' If you were talking on a one-to-one basis, you could talk through some problems ... as a mature student and also as a black student ... He'd say, 'You can make it through.

It's not a problem ...' [The fact that he was black] did make a difference to me. It helped. It was a bonus ... [He] actually looked at my unique problems that I had and was prepared to discuss them with me ... [It] was a positive thing ... But he seemed fair all around. And he was there when I needed him to kick my butt. To make sure that all the projects and essays were in on time.

(Sean, housing advice manager)

Neither Eve nor Zac attached much importance to the ethnicity of their benevolent individual. Both treated the fact that it was an Asian member of staff who encouraged them as incidental. But for Sean having a black tutor was 'a bonus'. That he described his tutor as someone he 'could have associated with usually' implies a strong identification. He was willing to discuss personal issues with this tutor and experienced a level of trust that no other participant experienced. Similarly, Zac described his relationship with the CAD technician as more of a friendship.

Observations in the literature (e.g. Allen, P., 1998; Reynolds, 2006) and in my participants' narratives suggest that white students receive more encouragement and develop closer relationships with white lecturers than their black peers do. In my research, black students who received extra support received it from minoritized staff. This may indicate a greater identification on grounds of race than is consciously acknowledged. However, it can leave black students at a disadvantage in accessing academic support because of the disproportionately low numbers of minoritized academic staff.

Paul Allen (1998) stresses the need to diversify the higher education curriculum by injecting more multicultural and anti-racist content, and this is echoed in the literature on race and education (e.g. Bird, 1996; Graham, 2001; Van Dyke, 1998; Acland and Azmi, 1998; Graham and Robinson, 2004). The dearth of African and Asian thinkers stimulated protests among SOAS (School of Oriental and African Studies, University of London) university students, who called for the UK's higher education curriculum to be decolonized (Mandhai, 2017). In September 2017 Birmingham City University launched the first Black Studies degree course in the UK, centring on black experiences and black contributions to society (BCU, 2017). But little attention is paid to black culture, authors, art, history or scientists in British universities and their exclusion perpetuates the continual reinforcement of racist, Eurocentric epistemology. 'Cultural domination has challenged economic exploitation as the fundamental social injustice', asserts Powell (1999: 20). This lack of black cultural content is an 'omission [that] renders black people and cultures invisible, and, by implication, less worthy of study. There has been little curriculum development in which non-European values and thought patterns are central' (Leicester and Merrill, 1999: 23).

My respondents overwhelmingly agreed that more multicultural activities and a multicultural core curriculum would enrich university life. Few felt that their course materials reflected the racial diversity of the UK or of the world. In particular, teacher training courses were heavily criticized for their inability to prepare future teachers for a multicultural school population, thus perpetuating the problem of poor teacher–student relationships and its negative consequences for black children. When race was discussed on the participants' courses, it was usually combined with gender and disability in a single session on diversity, which they considered grossly inadequate. Eve and Nora both studied for PGCEs (Postgraduate Certificate in Education) at prestigious universities and both were alarmed at the low priority given to the subject of race in their courses:

> In Islington, 68 per cent of the pupil population is non-white and then people are coming off courses, but they haven't done anything about anybody else's culture, about how to teach various cultures [or] about how different cultures react and work within the education setting ... Teachers are walking into a London school ... into a class that's got 90 per cent or even more non-white [pupils] and they haven't been taught anything. They could have come from Cornwall and walked into a school in the inner city and that's just ridiculous ... it really is, because that really is going to hinder the progress that the children make in terms of the teacher not being able to understand what's really going on with the children ... I mean on the PGCE I think they had a day, Equal Opportunities day or something, where you learned about everything – gender, race, social inclusion, everything.
>
> (Nora, headteacher)

The inadequate provision of diversity training within teacher training courses is evidenced by the fact that most newly qualified teachers feel ill equipped to deal with diversity in schools (Rhamie, 2007; Archer and Francis, 2007). It makes it easy for student teachers to draw on 'deficit models' of working-class children and families as the explanation for their low achievement (Gazeley and Dunne, 2005).

Paul Allen (1998) suggests that black students try to counter the Eurocentric bias of the mainstream higher education curriculum and build a sense of positive black identity through a 'black scepticality' that pursues their own histories and heroes, such as Gandhi and Malcolm X, as an extra-curricular activity. The reluctance of education policy makers to adopt true multiculturalism, instead of tacking a single token class about diversity on to the end of a course, is symptomatic of 'the fear that any de-centering of Western civilizations, of the white male canon is really an act of cultural genocide' (hooks, 1994; 32).

At the heart of this debate lies the issue of power. In the words of Young (1971):

> the granting of equal status to sets of cultural choices that reflect variations in terms of the [characteristics of the dominant group], would involve a massive redistribution of the labels 'educational' 'success' and 'failure', and thus also a parallel redistribution of rewards in terms of wealth, prestige and power.
>
> (Young, 1971: 38–9)

So the prevalence of middle-class values in education continues to silence black and working-class students in the classroom by casting them as 'others' (hooks, 1994). Reay (2001) notes that 'the working-class struggle for academic success is not about finding yourself but rather losing yourself in order to find a new, shiny, acceptable, middle-class persona' (Reay, 2001: 341).

Many students face the unhappy choice of being estranged from their roots or giving up their courses, and this is reflected in higher than average drop-out rates among working-class and minoritized students. Forms of dominance are, thus, perpetuated. hooks (1994) suggests that instead of acquiescing, students should challenge this status quo by persistently injecting their black and working-class perspectives, thereby changing the norms of the institution. In line with this stance and the monocultural curriculum, some participants creatively integrated a black perspective to their studies whenever feasible. Nora told me:

> There was nothing to do with black people on the Psychology degree ... I did my final year project [on] the education of a black child. So I specifically geared my project and my research towards black children. And similarly when you're given the options to do things on your course ... we had to do a module on behaviour and I did behaviour on black children; and we had to do one on parental involvement, I did black parents. And so I brought that in, because I was obviously very black conscious by then ...

but that was a choice ... and I think for some tutors it makes it uncomfortable for them.

(Nora, headteacher)

Nora's feeling that some lecturers were not entirely comfortable with matters of race was echoed by Eve:

> I did get into a conflict with one of the guys in the group. It was a piece that we had to read and he couldn't understand why I said it was racist and he was having a hard time with it. And I don't think the teacher dealt with it that well, even though I think she's a good teacher. She kind of drew it to a halt and then left it at that, instead of talking about it and getting us to explain 'Why is that racist?' And 'He's seeing it in that way and why are you reading it in a different way?' And I just don't think in the entire course that they celebrated ethnicity.

(Eve, entrepreneur/teacher)

Their tutors' discomfort can inadvertently silence minoritized students. Although some of my respondents saw the value of presenting a black perspective in their work, they were well aware of the risk. The black higher education students in Channer's research (1995) felt that they were marked more harshly when they wrote about issues relating to race. They highlighted that receiving low grades for essays that dealt with race was the personal cost of standing out and not conforming. The interviewees in my research who presented a black perspective in their work when they could felt that they were sometimes penalized for it, so were apprehensive lest it cost them marks:

> I think on one of the papers I got marked down for it. I'd taken the black perspective and I'd taken it quite strong and ... even though I knew what the quality of my work was, because I was mostly an A grade student in most of my essays and stuff and if anything I'd get a B. And they'd given me a C and I just thought, 'Oh it's because you didn't like what I was saying, it isn't anything to do with my style or the quality of it.'

(Nora, headteacher)

On the devaluing of black perspectives it is useful to apply Freire (1972). He argues that putting the words of the ruling class into the mouths of the oppressed is a '"digestive" concept of knowledge' (Freire, 1972: 26) that prevents the learner from speaking their own words about their own lived experiences. It denies that oppressed people can know for themselves, because the only knowledge they can legitimately convey is that which conforms to ruling-class ideology. Dean's sentiments were remarkably similar to Freire's:

> I was trying to overcomplicate it by writing all these essays using all these words that that particular course has caused you to use. And I thought, 'Here I go again, me changing my world to kind of fit in with this ... whatever they're asking from me.' And I thought, 'Well, it's only for a time. And then I can practise my way'. It's all interesting actually.
>
> (Dean, youth worker)

So although hooks (1994) advocates that black students should inject black perspectives so as to effect change in higher education, doing so may endanger their grades and relationships with lecturers. Students who are confident in their abilities are in a much stronger position than those who are not. It is an issue of cultural capital (Bourdieu and Passeron, 1994), an example of one of the multiple ways in which black voices are silenced in higher education institutions. Those who have had negative experiences of schooling and enter higher education from a non-traditional route – as is the case for many African-Caribbean and working-class students – may be at a particular disadvantage and find it more difficult to challenge the norm. The desire to fit in and just survive the experience is likely to prevail.

## Class and non-traditional students in higher education

Rollock *et al.* (2015) use Bourdieu's concept of capital to develop an incisive analysis of some of the complexities of social class for black professionals in Britain. The social class identity of my research participants was similarly complex. Many described elements of middle-class cultural capital in terms of attitudes and aspirations derived from their Caribbean parents, combined with working-class economic capital in terms of their family circumstances within the UK context. It is therefore important to examine the experiences of working-class as well as minoritized students in higher education.

Most students feel it is important to fit in and this is accentuated for non-traditional students, be they minoritized, working class or mature. African-Caribbean students in particular experience isolation in higher education (see, for example, Channer, 1995; Bird, 1996). Paul Allen (1998) documents the crucial role of informal black support networks in providing a safe and supportive environment for minoritized students who experience racism and a strong sense of isolation. Reynolds (2006) describes African-

Caribbean men as an invisible minority in higher education and observes that her respondents value education greatly, but express feelings of alienation and ongoing conflict between their lived experiences outside the institution and the values and norms within it. Feeling isolated is a major issue for these men, who describe their 'internal struggle' between 'university life' and 'real life' (Reynolds, 2006: 9). One of McKenley's (2005) 'seven black men' echoes these sentiments when he reflects on his parents' attitudes to his schooling, saying: 'There was a tension between wanting you to learn and recognising that education was having a disorienting effect for some children in trying to balance the Whiteworld and the Blackworld' (McKenley 2005: 138).

Before starting their higher education studies, most of my participants were anxious about possibly feeling isolated because of their age, class and race. So they elected to study close to home or black social networks, such as churches or family. They opted for institutions that had ethnically diverse student populations or were located in ethnically diverse cities. They imagined that isolation would be an inevitable part of studying in higher education but the reality was quite different because there were black social networks to link into. African-Caribbean Societies were central for several. Zac, for instance, was acutely aware of how few black students there were in his institution and glad to be able to mix with other black students:

> There must have been over a thousand people in the Art and Design campus, [but] a very, very, very, very small amount of black students ... When I started university it was just a means to an end and then I discovered the Afro-Caribbean Society and it was brilliant to me at the time. I was like, 'Wow, university ain't just about university, there's black people with the same type of experiences or going through the same type of thing.' So I always took part ... [and] I think it was comfortable to go through the university studies with that being around, even though I was quite local anyway. I didn't really move far away from home ... I think if it wasn't for the societies and being involved in things like ACFest[1] ... I would have just kinda ... Do you say, 'lose your blackness'? ... I do think if it wasn't for the societies I would have lost something.

> (Zac, entrepreneur)

Isolation and identity are closely linked. Reay (2001) notes that many working-class students fear being looked down on when they enter their higher education institution. Reay observes the paradox that students have to lose their working-class identity in order to find their academically successful self, which must be aligned to the middle-class values that permeate education: 'Their transcripts hint at a delicate balance between realizing potential and maintaining a sense of an authentic self' (Reay, 2001: 337).

Eve, a mature student in my cohort, alluded to this conflict when she contrasted the sense of belonging she felt on her Access course with the sense of isolation she experienced later:

> On the Access course I realized everyone was in the same boat and that put me at ease ... [But, the Russell Group[2] university I attended] was one where I really felt like a fish out of water initially, because I thought there were so many people that were quite snobby ... When I first went there we had to introduce ourselves and say which university we came from and I was like [post-1992[3] university name mumbled], because a lot of them had been to St Andrews and Oxford and I know it's wrong to put up these barriers, but I did think, 'I'm not going to get on with them.' They were from totally different backgrounds. And being the only black person in the group – yet again – you do have to gain these skills of how you're going to cope with it. I've tried not to shy away from who I am as a black person, but at the same time you know that the people that are around you don't really understand you. And so [it's] not that you put that bit to one side, but ... I know when I started at [the Russell Group university] I thought, 'Oh I can't suck my teeth [typical Caribbean expression of disdain] here,' but as I got to know the people more and got on well with them, I thought, 'Well, I'm not ashamed of who I am' and I even told some of them that I go home and do my hairdressing and I didn't care! And it didn't work against me, because I was true to who I was and I thought, 'I'm not trying to be something else.
>
> (Eve, entrepreneur/teacher)

Reay (2001) recognizes that class difference is at the root of her students' fear of being looked down on, but Eve's comments show that race compounds it for African-Caribbean students. She feared revealing 'characteristics of ethnicity' (Gillborn, 1990) such as sucking her teeth, and tried hard to conform and fit in. Zac described his discomfort at trying to fit in as a means to an end:

Industrial Design Engineering ... was absolutely right for me; spot on. That's what I thought just before I applied for it and during my first year. But that kind of thought started to diminish during the middle of my second year ... [I was] thinking, 'You know what, I'm not really being myself here. I'm just trying to fit in and it's not real' ... I knew I didn't fit in, but at the end of the day, I wasn't there to fit in. I was in there to try and get something for me.

(Zac, entrepreneur)

Zac also spoke about the ambiguity of no longer quite fitting in with his old friends:

[There] weren't direct barriers, but it was a bit frustrating at the time. Because I remember [my old friends] all had jobs and they were going out and they had money and ... there was me on my student [income] and ... I couldn't go to things ... And they never laughed at me, but I just kind of felt, 'Well, here I am [in higher education] ... knowing that I'm not comfortable ... And that's where I come from and there's my mates doing their things and having a great time, and I just felt that I was missing out.

(Zac, entrepreneur)

Fear of not fitting in connects with fear of failure or inadequacy and a surprisingly high number in my cohort expressed concerns about their own academic ability. Despite achieving the levels of education required to attend their courses, many were worried they might fail to meet the standards required and be less able than their peers. Eve graphically described her perception of the social stratification implied by university, positioning herself as unworthy despite her aptitude for study:

To be quite honest I've always felt ... that university is way up there and I'm way down there! Even though I've done all this study and loved it, I just thought it was way out of my reach ... I don't know if I thought as well, 'Will I have the ability or would I just make a mess of it?' I just lacked confidence.

(Eve, entrepreneur/teacher)

Michelle conveyed the same sense of trepidation intertwined with inferiority when she explained her rationale for attending a new university for her first degree and only then having the confidence to attend an old[4] university later to do her master's degree. Her understanding of the interconnection between social class and educational achievement was so deeply rooted that she, like Eve, doubted the evidence of her own academic achievements:

> I was very worried that I wasn't going to be able to make the grade ... I suppose I knew I wasn't stupid, I was always confident about my academic capabilities. I think I would have an inferiority complex being among middle-class children who had been geared up for that sort of education.
>
> (Michelle, teacher)

Reay (2001) attributes the anxieties of mature working-class students about their own ability to their negative school experiences and Reynolds (2006) reaches the same conclusion regarding the African-Caribbean male students in her research. For Reynolds' participants, the commonplace associations of African-Caribbean learners with poor educational outcomes added another layer of self-doubt.

It is important to acknowledge that participants' instincts about not fitting in are not imagined, or not only about their school experiences. For instance, Boliver (2013) identifies that black applicants to prestigious universities are less likely to be offered a place than their white counterparts with the same qualifications. Despite the perception of old universities being higher status, the evidence suggests that the teaching quality is not significantly better than that in new or teaching-focused universities (Boliver, 2015). So the choice of my participants to study in new universities, where they were more likely to feel welcome and obtain a similar quality of education, was quite logical.

Despite feeling inadequate when they entered higher education, all my participants succeeded in their undergraduate studies and most went on to postgraduate study. At that point an interesting gender dynamic emerged: it was the women who mostly went on to a master's degree.

## The gender dynamic of postgraduate studies

Within the anti-oppressive agenda of this research, I explored my participants' experiences of and attitudes to issues of gender in higher education. All believed that we need more female staff at various levels in universities.

Women form the majority of students in most subject areas at degree level, while men tend to favour work-related education and training (McGivney, 2004). This trend continues at postgraduate level, where women account for 55.6 per cent of students (ECU, 2014). Postgraduate study is a direct route to an academic career, but there is a complete reversal of the trend when it comes to teaching in higher education, with men occupying 55.5 per cent of academic posts and women only 44.5 per cent (ECU, 2014). Women academics are also concentrated in part-time employment on the lower rungs of the academic career ladder and under-represented in high-level posts. Just one in five professors is female (ECU, 2014).

The gender imbalance among higher education students mirrors the gender dynamic of postgraduate study in my research (see Table 4.1). Six of my ten participants obtained postgraduate certificates and diplomas. The men favoured these professional and work-related courses. Four of the five women, and just one of the five men, went on to complete master's degrees. What motivated the women to continue when the men did not?

McGivney (2004) finds that an intrinsic interest in their subject is an important motivation for studying for all learners, but men and younger students cite job-related reasons more frequently than women and older students. In my study, it is significant that in their questionnaire responses all the women but none of the men identified the pleasure of studying as a major motivation. For most of the men, studying in higher education was an exercise of willpower, undertaken for the extrinsic rewards associated with enhanced career prospects. While the women shared this utilitarian approach to the value of university, they were also motivated by an intrinsic desire to learn and a deeply felt love of their subject.

**Table 4.1:** Postgraduate qualifications

| Women | Professional/ job-related qualifications | Academic qualifications |
|---|---|---|
| Alison | Diploma in English Language Teaching to Adults (DELTA) | MA in English Language Teaching |
| Eve | PGCE | MA in Religion and Public Life |
| Michelle | PGCE | MSc in IT for Manufacture |
| Nora | PGCE | MA in Education Management |
| **Men** | | |
| Leroy | PGCE | |
| Neil | PG Diploma in Management Studies PG Diploma in Project Management | MA in Human Resources |

The link for the women between pleasure and learning stimulated their postgraduate study. They also expected it to improve their career prospects. Alison explained:

> The rationale behind doing the MA was because I missed study and I felt that I wasn't being intellectually challenged by the work. The teaching was there, but there wasn't any theory behind it ... So the MA came out of my own decision ... Work didn't suggest it [or] fund it. I asked for funding; it was refused ... I had to forgo pay, took less teaching hours and then had to do it in my own time. But I did feel that once I'd got the MA I could get a position of management and I could get the stable, full-time job in EFL [English as a foreign language] ... And I thought, 'Well [you'll have] your Master's and Diploma in EFL, you'll definitely land a job.'
>
> (Alison, HE lecturer)

In addition, the women who completed master's degrees all expressed interest in studying for a PhD. Freire (1996) uses critical pedagogy to analyse class dynamics in adult learning. Feminist pedagogy builds upon this, drawing attention to the gender dynamics: 'One of the main principles of feminist pedagogy is linking the struggles of equity espoused in the classroom with community struggles ... [and encouraging] students to actively engage in changing the structures that control women's lives' (Mogadime, 2003: 11).

The common theme among those who were interested in PhD studies was a desire to research issues within black communities and to explore the dynamics of race. Eve's research interest was black women and theology, Michelle's was black women in education and Nora's was black youth in Nottingham. The love of their subjects was their prime motivation. However, class dynamics, in terms of the opportunity cost of continued studies and particularly the loss of income, ultimately deterred them from further study.

Working-class women risk a poor return on their investment in higher education, because of their comparatively low earning power as graduates and their career orientation towards the community (Reay, 2003). Elias *et al.* (1997) found that men who graduate with PhDs in the social sciences go on to be higher earners, but this is not necessarily the case for women. The return on investment for women who graduate with master's degrees is much clearer than for those who go on to do a PhD. For the women in my research, the opportunity cost intensified as they progressed through their graduate studies and became a powerful barrier to an academic career.

Despite their ability and strong inclination towards academic endeavours, none pursued a PhD. This is interesting because all the interviewees felt there was a need for more female and black academics in higher education institutions. Eve commented:

> Well, quite a few people in my [master's degree] class are applying to do PhDs, because they want to be lecturers ... And I had a tutorial and I said that I'm going to do a PGCE afterwards. And [my tutor] said, 'Not a PhD?' And I said, 'No way!' He said, 'But you finished [your bachelor's degree] with a good first, didn't you?' which I had not told anybody. And I said, 'Yeeees' and he said, 'Soooo?' Then he said, 'What were you thinking of doing your PhD on?' So I began to tell him what I was going to do and because I just started rambling on about it he just said, 'Well, there's your PhD' ... I am drawn, but I need some money ... I need to work. It's horrible ... And I think probably because I've gone back as a mature student and this is my fifth year of study I'm just wearing thin. But I think if I'd done my degree younger [and finished at] 21 and [had] a bit more time ... Like some of my friends on this course are quite young as well. They're 21, 22, 23. So they've still got loads of time.
>
> (Eve, teacher/entrepreneur)

The strength of the women's love of learning led me to explore attitudes to postgraduate study and this revealed other barriers to higher education such as time and financial pressures. At the time of the interviews both Eve and Michelle were in their thirties and cited age as a deterrent to pursuing a PhD. There was a sense that time was running out and competing demands took priority:

> I would love to start doing my PhD ... [laughs] ... but I feel, because of [my] age I have to be sensible now, and doing a PhD isn't being sensible. It's almost harking back to my student days and not progressing ... I think when people stay within a job they might do their performance arts or sports after they've finished work, but in my free time I like discussing ideas ... In my ideal world I would find time to do my job very well, to be running a small business and to do my PhD and obviously to look after my children ... but now coming back to the real world I know that I can manage the job and I need to be successful at the job, because there is more riding on it than just money and I know my self-

esteem is linked up with my job ... also I know my children need me. So those are the two things that have priority ... I'd be willing to borrow the money to go and do a PhD. It's not the money factor any more, which used to be a key factor. It's the time factor.

(Michelle, teacher)

The balancing of childcare with career-related ambitions is a major issue for women who are primary carers and this, combined with the length of time, cost of study and loss of income while studying for the PhD, makes the pursuit of an academic career inaccessible to many African-Caribbean women. The intersections of race, class and gender dynamics are all too evident.

Given the opportunity, women such as these could be an asset, bringing their additional knowledge and experience of African-Caribbean culture to their higher education institutions. Professional black women gain empowerment and richness from their bicultural lifestyles, which combine the white, male-dominated culture that pervades most professions with the black culture of their origins (Bell, 1990). In the same way, black academics can bring their knowledge of academic culture to black communities, and their understanding of black cultures to the academic community, thus facilitating anti-racism and social inclusion (hooks and West, 1991). Arguably, 'Black women intellectuals best contribute to a Black women's group standpoint by using their experiences as situated knowers' (Collins, 2000: 19).

These findings suggest that an untapped opportunity exists for African-Caribbean women graduates to contribute their perspectives to the understanding of race, class and gender in UK higher education institutions. Ironically, it is the intersection of oppressions relating to those same characteristics of race, class and gender that creates an almost insurmountable barrier to African-Caribbean women's advancement.

## Conclusions

This chapter presented my research participants' experiences in higher education and explored the impact of staffing, curriculum and support networks. We saw that independent learning styles in higher education enabled these graduates to use emotional withdrawal as a strategy to manage difficult teacher–student relationships and fulfil their ambitions.

Many black students feel they receive less support from white staff than their white peers. In the rare instances that participants spoke of particularly supportive relationships, the support came from minoritized teaching staff. Respondents expressed the desire to see more black lecturers, who could both support black students and improve understanding between black students and white staff. The presence of minoritized academic staff breaks down some of the barriers raised by difference and appointing more would be proof of a commitment to equality.

The absence of diversity in the higher education curriculum was seen as a serious shortcoming and several participants injected a black perspective into their coursework when possible. However, this was risky in terms of the tension it could create in the classroom and the potential for being marked down. It is one of the multiple ways in which black voices are silenced within higher education.

Most of my participants were non-traditional students, concerned about fitting in and insecure about their academic ability. Black support networks were crucial to ease their sense of isolation.

It was predominantly the women who went on to complete master's degrees, stimulated by the pleasure of learning. Most of them considered studying for a PhD on issues pertaining to black communities, but the intersections of race, class and gender made the opportunity cost too great. Are these women an untapped resource in academic life that could research ways of voicing black women's standpoints? Their presence in academic careers would support social inclusion, and as Professor Tracey Reynolds has said: 'by just being visible ... scholars can see that you don't have to be white, male and from a middle-class background to become a professor' (Elmes, 2015). This would go some way to dismantling the white, middle-class, male hegemony that pervades higher education. But now we turn to the career destinations of participants.

## Notes

[1] Annual festival organized for and by members of African-Caribbean Societies from various higher education institutions.

[2] Russell Group universities are research led and are considered elite higher education institutions.

[3] Post-1992 or new universities tend to be teaching led and changed from polytechnic to university status in 1992.

[4] Old universities existed as universities prior to 1992 and are considered traditional and high status higher education institutions.

# Chapter 5

# Bitter sweet: Graduate careers

'Equality in education equals equality in life' is a widespread accepted principle that is disproved by the underemployment of Black graduates.

(BLINK, 2005: 12)

## Introduction

The lives of black professionals in the UK are relatively uncharted. Minoritized professionals and black women afford the closest focal points in the literature. This chapter contributes to the field by exploring the careers of black graduates.

My research participants experienced a bitter-sweet combination of success in gaining entry to professional careers and frustration at battling against oppressive organizational structures that constrained rather than developed them. All had embarked on professional careers that mostly combined public sector employment, entrepreneurialism and community service.

The number of the cohort pursuing careers in the public sector and teaching reflected a pragmatism linked to race, class and gender dynamics in employment and professional training opportunities in the UK. Once they had gained entry to professional occupations, race and gender created barriers to their progress within their organizations. Consequently, entrepreneurial endeavours appealed as a way of circumventing the organizational politics that impeded progress in their careers.

Their entrepreneurial inclination often intertwined with their community orientation. Many of their voluntary endeavours and entrepreneurial ideas involved community development initiatives that stemmed from a desire to improve conditions for black people in British society. These graduates also demonstrated their commitment to community service by working in institutions where they felt they could have a positive impact on black communities.

## Public sector careers

Black professionals are a largely invisible section of the population, frequently 'ignored by media, researchers and opinion makers' (Wingfield, 2011: ix). As the number of minoritized graduates in the UK grows, unemployment rates remain 'significantly higher for people from every ethnic minority when compared with White people' (EHRC, 2015: 37). In recent years, black people have experienced the biggest drop in pay rates and whereas minoritized graduates as a whole earn 10 per cent less than white graduates, black graduates earn a substantial 23 per cent less (TUC, 2016). In fact, the more qualified black employees are, the bigger the pay gap between them and similarly qualified white workers (TUC, 2016).

At the same time, girls and women outperform their male equivalents in education, but their careers do not reflect this. Women continue to earn less than men, are far more likely to be in part-time work and are concentrated in the lower-paid employment sectors (EHRC, 2015). Similarly, minoritized individuals are concentrated in some sectors of the job market and all but absent in others. For example, there is 'a lack of diversity in senior and managerial occupations (in terms of gender and ethnicity) ... and at board level in both the public and private sector' (EHRC, 2015: 99).

In her seminal research, Mirza (1992) identified that black girls were astute in selecting 'strategic careers', taking into account race and gender stratification within the UK employment market. They aspired to public sector careers such as nursing, social work and teaching, where there was a visible presence of minoritized people and women. An additional dynamic of large public sector employers is the priority given to equal opportunities, which reduces the discrimination experienced by minoritized people in the recruitment process. With caring still considered the domain of women (Hughes, 2002), and therefore remaining relatively low paid, the caring professions provide openings for women and black people to enter these lower-status and lower-paid professions.

Corresponding to the literature, Table 5.1 shows that nine of the ten participants were in public sector careers at some point during my primary research. Six were in the teaching profession and others in social services, housing and local government. Not one interviewee was employed within the private sector.

Although pay in the public sector tends to be lower than in the private sector, public sector careers have traditionally offered job security and this can be an attractive inducement for people who are well qualified but vulnerable in the job market. Public sector organizations are subject to higher levels of scrutiny than private sector organizations when it comes to demonstrating that they are equal opportunities employers and welcome diversity. This could account for the concentration of minoritized people in the public sector.

**Table 5.1:** Employment sector breakdown

| Name | Employment | Public/private sector |
| --- | --- | --- |
| Elaine | Local government consultant/self-employed | Public/private |
| Nora | Headteacher (school) | Public |
| Michelle | Teacher (school) | Public |
| Eve | Teacher (school)/self-employed | Public/private |
| Alison | Lecturer (HE) | Public |
| Leroy | Lecturer (FE) | Public |
| Neil | Lecturer (FE)/IT trainer | Public/public |
| Dean | Youth worker | Public |
| Sean | Housing advice manager | Public |
| Zac | Self-employed | Private |

However, the increasing privatization and austerity measures taken by successive governments have significantly eroded the public sector. While women are likely to be most affected by public sector job cuts (McKay *et al.*, 2013), minoritized workers 'have been disproportionately affected by the growth in part-time, insecure and low-paid employment' (TUC, 2015a: 3). These are some of the key characteristics of the newly emerging class called the 'precariat' – and they are particularly vulnerable in the employment market (Savage, 2015).

Much of the literature addressing race and education calls for more black teachers (e.g. Education Commission, 2004; BLINK, 2005), so I was surprised to find so many participants in the teaching profession. Teaching appeared to be the default career. Funding for a PGCE is more accessible than for most postgraduate courses and a PGCE offers a structured, direct route into graduate employment after one year of postgraduate study. So it is an attractive and accessible career choice for people with little economic capital.

This was the case for some of my cohort: Michelle, for example, recounting her rude awakening when the flood of job offers she had envisioned at the end of her degree course did not materialize. For pragmatic reasons she embarked on a PGCE. Eve, on the other hand, had completed a teaching certificate in an FE college many years before studying for her degree and was unimpressed by her first experience of teaching. Nevertheless, after completing her bachelor's and master's degrees, she applied for a PGCE as a kind of security blanket:

> I did the City and Guilds 7307 Teacher Training course … It was very trying. I always vowed I'd never go into teaching after … [Then after graduating] I was just hoping to apply for the PGCE, not knowing if teaching was for me – even though I'd hated it the first time. I just [wanted] to get the qualification, so I could actually have a profession.
>
> (Eve, entrepreneur/teacher)

Similarly, Leroy completed a PGCE, but did not enjoy teaching in school, so was reluctant to pursue a teaching career. He considered teaching a 'soft option' until, after several years of disappointment in his chosen career, he was pleased to secure a teaching post at an FE college. He described his journey back into teaching:

> [Last year] I was mainly at home and doing some temping; carpentry and stuff … and then I ended up doing some sales work and I was trying to make ends meet. I … got a bit desperate for some money … it was just convenient … [Then] I was contacted near the end of the summer for the position that I've got now lecturing in a college … I didn't really want to get back into teaching. Not school teaching anyway. I never really thought I'd get the position I've got, which is something that I really wanted to do straight after I finished college. And now I've got it and it's not as great, because I'd have liked to get it when I was 22. So it's come [way] too late … my idea was to sort of teach part time and do my own stuff on the side and that's still my ideal. Actually, my ideal is doing my own stuff all the time and not having to worry about money, but it's not realistic, especially in my field … I'm just being realistic. Unless you're really lucky or you've got the right sort of contacts … it's really who you know not what you know in the Arts.
>
> (Leroy, FE lecturer)

Other interviewees were en route to something else when a teaching career became a more attractive option. Nora, for instance, entered teaching with the intention of gaining the two years of teaching experience she needed to pursue a career as an educational psychologist. However, she developed a love of teaching and excelled in her teaching career, becoming a headteacher in her early thirties. Alison, having struggled with her first choice of degree course, faced a crossroads and decided that teaching English as a Foreign Language (EFL) would allow her to pursue her love of language and travel the world:

> When I knew that I was going to fail [my Speech Therapy degree] I thought, 'What am I going to do?' I still liked languages and linguistics, so then I thought of English as a Foreign Language. I thought I could teach that. I had this inner desire to prove myself linguistically, because I didn't have a qualification that reflected my interest in language or linguistics. So I said, 'Right, if you do a TEFL [Teaching English as a Foreign Language] course, that will show that you can still do linguistics and then you can go away, you can travel the world.' You know, not so stressed out.
>
> (Alison, HE lecturer)

Teaching attracts large numbers of women. Their numbers in primary schools and the lower levels of the profession is associated with the caring nature of the career. Professionally qualified women also gravitate towards teaching because it fits relatively well with childcare commitments. One might expect women's increasing activity in the employment market over recent decades to correspond with a reduction in their roles as primary carers within the family but this is not so (Omar *et al.*, 2004). Women carry 80 per cent of caring and domestic responsibilities in the UK (DTI, 2003). A teaching career with school holidays can allow mothers of school-age children to juggle their work and childcare responsibilities effectively.

Michelle did a master's degree immediately after finishing her PGCE. Her (predominantly white, male) peers were destined for lucrative careers in industry, but she had her first child soon after completion, so a teaching career became a more viable option. Similarly, Elaine considered retraining for a teaching career during the period of the research, so she could balance family and work commitments but she eventually opted for self-employment. Many women face a similar dilemma when making career choices at a time in their lives when childrearing becomes a priority. Michelle explained:

> I want to stay in teaching. When my children are off I can be off. And I can manage my time a lot more ... I'm sticking with it, because it's family orientated, not necessarily because I'm thinking this is a wonderful career and what I wanted to do.
>
> (Michelle, teacher)

Motherhood is still one of women's primary roles (Hughes, 2002) and careers constitute an important part of people's identities. Consequently, a significant number of graduate and professional women go into part-time employment after having children, in an attempt to balance their caring responsibilities and their careers. This undermines their earning potential. Working-class women who study as mature students run the added risk of failing to gain a return on their investment in adult education (Reay, 2003) because their earning capacity as graduates is not enough to compensate for their loss of earnings while studying.

The combined impact of poor childcare provision in the UK (Prowess, 2005) and a system that takes no heed of the family commitments of workers is that many mothers, including graduates, find themselves in work that is relatively low paid, low status and part time. It is still the case that:

> [t]he social reality women have to face is that motherhood and paid employment are objectively incompatible in a world that puts the isolated nuclear family (the American dream unit) against the capitalist organisation of work in Western industrial society.
>
> (Joseph and Lewis, 1986: 129)

During the three years of my primary research, Michelle went through several part-time teaching posts, trying to juggle work and childcare, but was mindful of her loss of earning power. She described how she would work a few hours to fit in with her family commitments, only to discover that she could not earn enough to cover childcare costs. She was candid about needing to work, rather than staying at home full time:

> It was difficult, because [the job] wasn't really paying for my childcare, but I wanted to stay at work. Actually there was part of me that needed to stay at work ... because I'm one of those people that work defines me ... I felt like I had given everything up to be in this relationship. I felt almost like I'd become some sort of automaton ... and having one foot in the world of work, I just felt like I hadn't totally gone under ... so I just needed to stay in work.
>
> (Michelle, teacher)

Despite large numbers of women and growing numbers of minoritized people in the teaching profession, their numbers diminish according to how high up the organizational hierarchy they are – the top posts remain dominated by white men. In terms of gender, this is hardly surprising in light of Nora's hectic lifestyle as a headteacher and mother. Nora said she worked 50 to 60 hours a week. She sometimes ran two schools and she also ran a part-time course in higher education, developing black teachers for leadership roles. She was the lone parent and primary carer for two school-aged children and bought in home help to make this possible:

> [I used to work] at least 60 [hours a week on a regular basis]. But ... I stopped that. The latest I leave here now is 7.30 p.m. ... It's a long week, but ... this is the lightest it's ever been; the [least] I've ever worked, because I hardly ever work on weekends any more and that's made a lot of difference as well ... I feel this is the right balance now. Even in the Easter holidays I only worked one day, which is really unheard of. I usually have to work at least four or five days in any holiday ... And nearly every day now, from 9 p.m. till 10 p.m., I can watch a programme and that's like luxury. I really kind of feel spoilt that I can watch some TV every night.
>
> (Nora, headteacher)

In spite of teaching initially providing a safe haven in which participants could utilize their skills in professional employment, all but one of the respondents were cynical about their teaching careers. Neil summed up:

> I really loved it at first, and then over the years it's just changed.
>
> (Neil, IT trainer)

## Glass ceilings and sticky floors

The term 'glass ceiling' describes the invisible ceiling typical of organizations that prevent women from climbing to the high levels of the corporate ladder. Nelson (2004) similarly uses the term 'sticky floor syndrome' to describe the situation where prejudice keeps minoritized women down at the bottom of their professions. When it comes to race, it is not only women who face prejudice: the term 'ethnic penalty' encapsulates 'all sources of disadvantage that may lead an ethnic group to fare less well in the labour market than do similarly qualified white people' (Modood *et al.*, 1997: 144).

The ethnic penalty is characterized by longer qualifying periods in education, attendance at lower-status educational institutions and discrimination in job applications (Mayor, 2002). The degrees gained by minoritized graduates are devalued and once employed in an organization they tend to languish at the bottom of the career ladder and have to move sideways into other organizations to progress (Reynolds, 1997). Was this the case for my cohort?

At the end of the primary research, eight of the ten participants were employees and two were self-employed. Of the employees, only one – Nora – had made significant progress in her career and maintained a senior position since she entered her chosen profession, suggesting that she was the exception rather than the rule. Despite several years in graduate employment in their chosen fields, Alison, Michelle, Sean, Leroy and Neil were all frustrated that their careers seemed to plateau at an early stage. Indeed, most of the participants in employment, rather than self-employment, said they were frustrated with their careers.

After several years in her job on various part-time, temporary contracts, Alison decided to complete a self-funded master's degree so her career would progress at last:

> I started the MA and loved it. I just thought, 'All this knowledge,' and 'Gosh there's so much about the language … I just love it … I really liked doing the MA and then the dissertation was in second language acquisition, which is the area that I really like. So I passed all the modules and then was quite happy when I got a distinction in the dissertation … And so I had this MA now and still in the job, but now I feel I'm not using my MA skills as such in this job. And the way I feel about teaching now is that at first I was very interested in imparting this language knowledge to students and I was quite happy to do the analysis and the lesson preparation behind it, because it was the manipulation of language that I liked to do … but now the teaching side is not a challenge at all any more.
>
> (Alison, HE lecturer)

Her enthusiasm about her subject was clear, but even with her relevant qualifications and eight years of teaching her subject, the desired promotion did not materialize.

## The women's careers

Nora's career progress was quite linear. Something of a pioneer, she became one of the youngest headteachers in her borough – and in the UK – in her early thirties. At headteacher meetings she was usually the only black person and one of the few women to have risen to that level in teaching.

Similarly, Elaine made good career progress, by moving through a range of organizations rather than gaining promotion internally. Her employers were public sector and non-government organizations. She then moved into self-employment, to avoid the organizational politics and create a manageable work/life balance with her family.

Eve's career was in a period of transition. After running her own successful hairdressing business for some years, she was about to embark on a career in teaching. However, having recently completed retraining, she was already expressing reservations about the career move.

Michelle's and Alison's teaching contracts were not secure. Their frustration over their careers resonates with the literature. Both felt that people dynamics had hindered their progress and Michelle was certain that racism played a part. Like Elaine, she was mindful that her career choices had to be balanced against the priority of childcare commitments.

## The men's careers

Zac had been running his successful business in multimedia promotions since shortly after he graduated. Dean, a youth worker, was quite casual about his career progression as an employee and focused on entrepreneurial endeavours as the way forward. Sean, Neil and Leroy were, to a large extent, disappointed with how their careers were progressing.

Sean expressed concerns about his career path since graduation when I asked him:

Amanda:     How do you feel generally about your career progression since graduation? Are you pleased with it? Are you frustrated with it? Has it gone better than you'd anticipated?

Sean:     It's not gone any better ... It's got a foot in the door, but it hasn't overcome the same prejudices that were there in the first place. It's allowed me to get into this position, but even so it hasn't given me that much of a leg up, because there are people in my position who haven't got a degree. All the black people in my position have got degrees, but not all the white people; in fact [it's quite uncommon]. So I don't really see it giving me that big a leg up. Although I needed it in order to gain the trust, otherwise I don't think I would have got the post. But in a sense of being respected any more within the workforce, not really. Not really. Whether it's your peers, subordinates or managers, you don't get it. You don't get it at all.

Sean was well aware of the ethnic penalty he was paying in his career. He reasoned that, as a black man, he needed a degree in order to gain 'trust' and get a job that did not actually require a degree. He had to be overqualified.

He was certain that without his degree he would never have been able to secure his job. The underemployment of minoritized workers (TUC, 2015a) and the disparity between the education levels of his black and white colleagues corroborated Sean's belief. Wright *et al.* (2007) discussed this issue of trust and examined how power networks operate to exclude black workers and subject them to high levels of surveillance.

Neil, by contrast, was reluctant to cite race as a hindrance to his career progression. He acknowledged the existence of racism and even his own experiences, but said he preferred not to confront it as an issue. He had been frustrated in his previous employment, when many of his younger, less qualified colleagues in the industry had climbed the ladder into management by networking, but networking had not worked for him. He attributed this to chance misfortune and decided to consider a career change:

> But I want to get back into project management. Because when I left teaching … after about nine years, I moved to a software company as a Training Consultant. And then I got bored of training [and] moved into [IT and finance] project management, because planning and organizing etc. is something I really like. Then I was made redundant … So since then I've been back in teaching part time and picking up contracts as and when. But one thing I did find actually … when I worked for the company, a lot of the managers were younger than me and didn't have half as many qualifications as me. A lot of them didn't even have a bachelor's [degree]. They worked on experience. And this is what concerns me with education. Before I used to always tell [my students] that they should get qualifications, but now I'm not so sure.
>
> (Neil, IT trainer)

Although Neil did not concede that race was relevant, his experience echoed that of many black professionals, who struggle to climb organizational hierarchies and have to change jobs in order to progress. He described the cyclical nature of his career progression and recounted how years of frustration while teaching in further and higher education led him to leave the profession:

> I don't feel I've gone around in circles, but it's not that straightforward. It certainly hasn't been easy. I do feel I've progressed. I mean, until I was made redundant, that's what sort of knocked me back … It gave me a chance to do contract work,

but then that's dried up … I'd been teaching for so long, which is fine and I didn't really get to where I wanted and that doesn't particularly bother me. And I left and I'm happy with that; that I left. I talked about it and I did it.

(Neil, IT trainer)

After a period of not working, Neil was relieved to secure employment as an IT trainer in a London local authority that employed large numbers of black staff. He expressed regret at the level of the job he had managed to get. His hopes for developing his new role ended in disappointment and a sense of being unable to utilize his skills and potential.

## Vulnerability and outsider status

In addition to a general sense of being stuck, many participants were subject to official or unofficial disputes at work. In Sean's case, this culminated in him being suspended on the basis of a false allegation. He was ultimately cleared of the allegation, which he described as bizarre, and the way managers had dealt with him was proved to be inappropriate. However, the union refused to support him in pursuing a grievance:

I was suspended because of an allegation from a tenant … [Considering] the lack of evidence, they obviously took their account very, very seriously … Before they'd even queried me they'd already made the decision to suspend [me] … They say it's the standard procedure, but apparently it wasn't … but in the end the union said that they wouldn't support me in taking out a grievance.

(Sean, housing advice manager)

Many black workers feel unsupported by their union when they try to tackle racism or disputes within the workplace (Robinson, 2007), and the introduction of tribunal fees 'are creating barriers for BME [black and minority ethnic] workers to be able to seek redress when faced with exploitation and discrimination at work' (TUC, 2015a: 12). In spite of significant evidence that the matter had been mismanaged, Sean felt compelled to give up fighting his grievance, because of the financial and personal cost of pursuing it alone. During his suspension, his managers had sought to build a bigger case against him by delving into the past and trying to discredit him with more unfounded and unsubstantiated accusations:

They [started] looking at general things relating to my conduct and trying to bring in other things … But they were trying to

cover ... I think they then were just looking for something for a
viable reason to suspend me.

(Sean, housing advice manager)

Sean was adamant that racism played a part in his case and reasoned
that the organization was going through a privatization process and had
an unspoken strategy to get rid of employees before the changeover. He
highlighted the large number of black workers under suspension and
maintained that they were an easy target:

> There's always a racial dynamic. It's just how it is. At the time
> there must have been four or five people of colour that were
> suspended and it was a time just before the changeover and I
> don't know whether they were trying to discourage people from
> coming over to the new [organization]. I think there was only one,
> [maybe two] who were subsequently sacked ... The others were
> reinstated. I know people who there was no case to answer, so
> they just came back ... The management team has been criticized
> by the Audit Commission and Best Value Team.

(Sean, housing advice manager)

During an appraisal, Alison had agreed to seek extra responsibility for
career development within her current role. She described the battle that
later ensued. Like Sean's, her manager tried to undermine her by actively
seeking evidence to discredit her in order to promote a less experienced and
less qualified white colleague to the position:

> I had to fight for [additional responsibility] ... The frustration
> was that the person that did not want me to do it was in charge
> of that particular course and she had gone into files and tried to
> seek out if there were any complaints [about me] from students
> ... She wanted to prove [my] incompetence, [because] she wanted
> her friend to have the position ... This friend had no diploma,
> less experience than myself, but she wanted to give him that
> opportunity ... So she went to the organizer who is above her to
> discuss, 'I don't want Alison to do this'. And she must have said,
> 'Is there anything else?' because she would not have had access
> to files on me. So [she] and the person above her got together, set
> out an agenda for this meeting [and] I was totally unaware that
> they were going to bring up these two issues. I thought I was just
> going in to talk about my ideas for module leadership and then
> went in and found out that they had plotted, colluded together,

not to promote staff development, but to keep me down. So I had
to fight and battle through that.

(Alison, HE lecturer)

The search for reasons to prevent Alison from progressing proved fruitless.
In the absence of ammunition, her manager reluctantly agreed to give her
new responsibilities that might further her career. But the emotional cost
of being undermined by colleagues was immeasurable and Alison's love of
her job was tainted by the negativity she felt about her work environment.
She deduced that not being a member of the right clique was at the root of
her problem.

Participants rarely related their negative experiences in organizations
to overt racism and tended to see it as covert racism or as the result of
being an outsider. In a racialized context, few black employees manage to
secure professional or senior positions, so those who do can face isolation
in their careers and a degree of detachment from their communities (hooks,
1993). The literature on bicultural lifestyles (see Bell, 1990; McKenley,
2005; Gilkes, 1982) explores how black professionals juggle the demands
of predominantly white, middle-class, male-oriented organizational
cultures with their own cultural backgrounds that may be embedded in
disenfranchised black communities. Gordon (2007) uses Du Bois' (2000
[1903]) 'double consciousness' when discussing bicultural competence
and is emphatic about the need for black professionals to address internal
conflicts that can arise from this duality. Alfred (1997) uses Collins's (1986,
2000) 'outsider within' concept to explain the 'creative marginality' that
black women academics use to successfully move between the spheres of
their professional and personal lives.

Not quite fitting into an organization's 'old boy network' can
undermine career progression for women and black staff. The isolation of
being the only black person in a senior position can create added pressure
to succeed, and damage their emotional wellbeing. Paul Allen (1998)
reasons that because of negative racial stereotyping, many black students
feel the need to succeed on behalf of their race when they are in an isolated
and esteemed position. The theory of tokenism identifies similar issues
in the careers of black professionals, who experience hyper-visibility and
invisibility in their predominantly white work environments (Wingfield,
2011). Black professionals are highly visible if they make a mistake or if
issues of race come to the fore. Conversely, they often experience invisibility
and isolation when it comes to accessing professional social networks that

can enhance their career progress. Nora spoke about her experience of isolation and pressure to succeed:

> Even now as a headteacher ... in [a London borough] I'm the only black headteacher and I'm the youngest headteacher and when I walk into ... headteachers' meetings, that's the thing that's always with me. I'm the only black person here. And it puts pressure on me, because the African-Caribbean children are the worst-performing ones in the borough and so anything that's going on, I always feel like, '[Nora], all eyes are on you. You're the only African-Caribbean person ... the only black person, even, in this room. There's not even another African person.' And I'm under constant pressure ... because all the spotlights are going to be on me. You know, 'She's a black headteacher, talking about role models. How are the black children doing in her school then?' [So] I feel like I can't fail, because I'd be failing the whole race. That can be a pressure.
>
> (Nora, headteacher)

Nora was mindful that being labelled the 'race expert' could detract from her other attributes and lead to further marginalization:

> Sometimes I don't speak out the way that I would want to, because I'm the only black person there and I just think, I don't want to be, 'Oh Nora's on her race card again,' because then when you want to say things about other things they won't take you seriously ... It's a lonely cry ... They do call me about race things [and] I've taken myself off to do this [course], which is about black people, because I love it and I do feel that's within my comfort zone. But I also need to make sure that I stay within things like data and finance ... I need to stay in all those key areas, so that I'm not just sidelined to doing black things.
>
> (Nora, headteacher)

Eve discussed the impact of being the only black person in educational and work environments and described the added comfort she felt when she was working with another African-Caribbean woman and could feel free to bring her cultural norms to the work environment without fear of reprisals or negative judgements:

> I'm getting fed up of being the only black person in a lot of situations; not only education, but also in certain church

committees ... And you do have to gain these skills of how you're going to cope with it ... I've tried not to shy away from who I am as a black person, but at the same time the people that are around you ... don't really understand you as a black person ... So you do feel like, not that you put that bit to one side, but like at work at the moment with [Sharon] I can start bussing out with patois [speaking in Caribbean dialect]. We both do it with each other, but before I was there she wouldn't have had anyone to do that with. So for both of us it's really great support. And a lot of her friends outside of teaching are saying, '[Sharon] is really going to miss you.' And I think it's things like that. Because we can have a really good banter and we're sucking our teeth [in disdain] and that kind of stuff, where you know you've still got it, it's still there, you still know about who you are as a black person, but before I came there she wouldn't have had anyone to be like that with.

(Eve, entrepreneur/teacher)

Eve felt a sense of belonging when she could express herself freely and reveal parts of her identity as an African-Caribbean by speaking patois. She contrasted her sense of having to dumb down that part of her identity when she was in an all-white work or education environment – and not just because white people did not understand it, but because they considered it unacceptable. Sean gave examples of how his organization regarded African-Caribbean behaviour norms as subversive:

Sean:    There's lots of black people at my office and so we do kind of relax a bit, but it's not in a sinister way. But still some of the people in the office take offence and say, 'Oh you shouldn't be talking patois, because we don't understand what you're saying ...' And we're saying, 'No, don't take it in the wrong way ... this is our [way of being]' ... They just don't like it at all, because we just seem to be having too much fun ... because that's what they complain about. They say, 'Ooh, people can see you at the counter and you're laughing and joking' ... and [we're] saying 'Well, what's wrong with laughing and joking?' ... as long as they're getting the service and you don't go over the top.

Amanda:     And it looks unprofessional, too many black people laughing in the office. You can't be doing your work, can you? [Laughs]

Sean:       Exactly! That's it, exactly.

In Chapter 2 on schools, Michelle similarly observed that her teaching assistant treated African-Caribbean children's behaviour with suspicion when Michelle was teaching. Despite evidence to the contrary, he interpreted their joviality as an indication that they were not working. The dominance of white, middle-class norms in schools and workplaces and the white teachers' and managers' lack of cultural awareness curtail and label African-Caribbean norms of behaviour as deviant. Reay (2002) quotes Bourdieu to illuminate working-class experiences of education thus: 'when habitus encounters a social world of which it is the product, it is like a "fish in water": it does not feel the weight of the water, and it takes the world about itself for granted' (Bourdieu and Wacquant, 1992: 127). For African-Caribbean students and employees in the UK, the experience can be more akin to the 'fish out of water'. It is a daily struggle to survive in an environment that is not conducive to their wellbeing.

    To succeed in education and then in the workplace, African-Caribbean people often have to alter their behaviour to fit in. However, this is not without cost and '[people] managing diverse professionals and HRM [human resource management] specialists need to recognize how much identity work (e.g. frequently countering stereotyping) has to be done by black professionals in cultures that do not value diversity' (Atewologun and Singh, 2010: 332). Bell (1990) found that professional African-American women experienced their black networks as empowering and supportive, but felt at risk and cautious within their predominantly white, work-oriented networks. They had a strong sense that they were only just acceptable:

> They are extremely vigilant in their work environments, and they take pain in not revealing parts of their true selves ... the women don't feel safe emotionally ... there is a sense of distrust.
>
> (Bell, 1990: 474)

Alison's and Sean's experiences of managers who actively sought information to discredit them indicate that this vulnerability is not imagined. Their status is as tenuous as unwanted guests at someone else's table. Sean observed:

> It is partly to do with the racial dynamic, but it's unprofessional because they show favouritism. They're not impartial. So if it's a black person they'll follow that issue, whereas if it's a white

person they won't necessarily pursue [it]; they'll deal with it informally. That's the environment ... but you just have to grin and bear it ... It's a fairly good wage in [local] terms, but in terms of what it does to your soul, it's destroying you ... You can't put a price on your soul, can you?

(Sean, housing advice manager)

Black professionals who, despite their achievements, face continued discrimination in employment and life can feel suppressed rage (hooks, 1996). Although in the USA there are formalized strategies to assuage the anger and frustration that arise from experiencing racism in careers (McKenley, 2005), such strategies are glaringly absent in the UK:

> The US strategies include: the development of conflict resolution competencies to enable individuals to handle the racism they will inevitably experience as they develop careers, and skill-building programmes which help individuals to manage their 'rage' over the experience of racism ... they are organisationally based, suggesting a shared responsibility between the organisation and the individuals of black and minority ethnic heritage. This contrasts markedly with the UK experience where their race experiences seem to be something ethnic minorities are expected to work on individually.

(McKenley, 2005: 158)

In the UK there are growing numbers of black support networks, particularly in those professions that have large numbers of black staff, such as social services. Also, legislation has evolved so that, for example, the Race Relations Act was amended to acknowledge the subtlety of racism by giving weight to the complainant's perception of discrimination alongside the bare facts. Nonetheless, the evidence from my research suggests that the additional problem of racism in employment persists for black professionals. In the face of these difficulties, growing numbers of black women in the UK consider either emigration or setting up their own businesses as an alternative to battling through the organizational politics that plague their graduate careers (BBC Radio 4, 2006). The next section will explore this phenomenon in relation to my research participants.

## Entrepreneurialism

Entrepreneurialism is providing an alternative for increasing numbers of black workers and women who face obstacles in the workforce (Nelson,

2004; Maurey, 2005; Wingfield, 2011). The changing UK labour market has brought a general growth in self-employment (Purcell, 2000) and since the 2007–8 economic crash about half of the growth in women's employment has been self-employment (TUC, 2015b). Increasing numbers of minoritized women have started up businesses of their own and in 2005 the London Development Agency identified that 29 per cent of black women in London owned businesses, making them the most likely among women to set up their own enterprise (LDA, 2005). At the same time, in the USA self-employment is on the rise among black workers and 'black women constitute the largest group of new business owners' (Wingfield, 2011: 27).

Entrepreneurialism surfaced as a strong theme during the interviews about careers. Five of the interviewees had been fully self-employed and a further three partially self-employed at some time during their career. So a total of eight of my ten participants had been entrepreneurs and all those who no longer worked for themselves expressed a career aspiration to return to self-employment. Their business ventures, represented in Table 5.2, included hairdressing, printing, consultancy, coaching, furniture design, private tutoring, multimedia promotions, alternative therapy and property management.

**Table 5.2:** Self-employment

| Name | Occupation/industry | Full-/Part-time |
| --- | --- | --- |
| Elaine | Management consultant | Full-time |
| Eve | Hairdresser; property management | Full- and part-time |
| Michelle | Private tutor | Part-time |
| Dean | Alternative therapist; property management | Part-time |
| Leroy | Furniture designer | Full- and part-time |
| Neil | Coach | Part-time |
| Sean | Printer | Full-time |
| Zac | Multimedia promotions | Full-time |

Self-motivation, determination and drive are characteristics associated with entrepreneurs and the participants displayed these attributes throughout the research. The literature suggests that male entrepreneurs are likely to be risk takers and that successful networking is a strong characteristic among female entrepreneurs (Nelson, 2004). Nelson (2004) argues that women are the single most untapped human resource and that encouraging business start-ups among them could provide a route out of poverty for large numbers of women. Similarly, Barclays (2005) acknowledges the contribution that enterprises run by minoritized people make to the UK economy and their potential to promote economic inclusion by generating social and financial capital. Their research identified that minoritized entrepreneurs were more likely than others to be professionally qualified or graduates. Their key motivators were the 'desire to be their own boss', 'independence' and 'making money'. Compared with employees, 'The self-employed are [also] more likely [than employees] to ... have high levels of job satisfaction and happiness' (Blanchflower and Shadforth, 2007: 257).

My respondents had taken various routes into self-employment, but a few patterns emerged. The first cluster were young entrepreneurs, who launched their first businesses in their twenties after just a few years of working in their chosen fields. Sean, Eve and Zac had no business background or mentors to guide them through the business start-up process, but their drive and motivation stood them in good stead.

Sean left school with few qualifications and after a period as a trainee electrician he moved into the print business:

> I worked for a printers ... Did that for maybe four, five years ... and then started my own printing business ... I found it hard first of all getting finances. I knew very little about what it took to run a business, other than the few bits and bobs that I'd read for myself, but then I just decided to go for it really. Had a bit of advice from a friend that was also in printing ... And I got a couple of reasonable contracts. And people came to work for me, but although I could get the contracts in, it's getting the money and having the leverage to deal with some of the larger clients in terms of getting the money in once you'd done the job ... It wasn't doing fantastic, but it was ticking along.
>
> (Sean, housing advice manager)

After a few years Sean went into partnership with a friend, but within a matter of months the business folded and he went through a 'period of rediscovery' that took him back into education.

Eve's transition to self-employment followed a few years of employment in a popular hair salon:

> When I left [Slick Salon] I was 21 ... I just had these great ambitions of working for myself ... So at the age of 21, I decided to go into my first business venture, which was to have my [own] salon in town. And it felt absolutely fantastic. I had to work really

hard ... But even when I look back then the rent was ... high, but
I probably had more money in the bank then than I have now.

(Eve, entrepreneur/teacher)

In her thirties Eve was still running a successful business as a mobile
hairdresser while pursuing a number of part-time and then full-time
academic qualifications. Having recently completed teacher training and
her first year of teaching, she was contemplating continuing in business.
Her entrepreneurial spirit was indomitable:

> I love working for myself. Not just in hairdressing, but I am a
> hard worker and I think it gives you that buzz to learn things
> for yourself and do things for yourself. It makes you more
> independent ... It's brilliant; freedom.

(Eve, entrepreneur/teacher)

Despite the disapproval of his lecturers, Zac's astute business acumen led
him to develop his skills in Computer Aided Design (CAD) while he was
studying for his degree. His livelihood is now dependent on those skills. He
reflected:

> I met people that had actually done [my] course [and] the majority
> of them weren't working, even though they were really good ...
> So I said to myself, 'I'm going to have to do something that's
> going to get me a job.' Now at the time I noticed that looking
> at the ads for industrial designers it all came back to this so-
> called CAD/CAM, which we weren't being taught. We were being
> taught traditional skills, but not really computer-based design.
> We had a great CAD facility at the place and nobody was using
> it to do design. I [thought] ... I'm going to have to learn this thing
> against what the tutors were saying. This is why certain tutors
> turned against me, because they saw that I was still doing my
> course, but doing this other thing as well. And presenting my
> work in a non-traditional way. So when it came to my final year,
> the majority of my work was computer based, using multimedia
> technology ... And when I left polytechnic, I realized that there
> was this kind of buzz word going on – multimedia – [and I]
> realized [I'd] done a bit of that ... So [I thought] let me try and
> pursue seeing what this multimedia thing is about. So, I put my
> portfolio on a floppy [disk, an early type of computer portable
> storage device] and it was interactive. So you could see my
> work, there was sound, there was a Curriculum Vitae; basically

a presentation on a floppy. That was ten years ago. I sent that around to several agencies and I had phenomenal response really, because it was like, 'What is this! A presentation on a floppy!' So I got a lot of work from that. And people coming back saying, 'Look, do this for my company.' And I started to do that on a freelance basis ... I got some work from some ad agencies, and then working on some large campaigns and stuff. But then I took a step back and thought, 'You know what, you're setting up too much people here. I'm doing alright out of it, but there's also an opportunity here to do your own thing.' So, [me and my business partner] set up and then from there it's just gone on. Multimedia, literally ... it's happening, it's here and now. You can't go through a day without seeing some interaction, whether it's video, touch screen information, even using a cashpoint.

(Zac, entrepreneur)

The second cluster of entrepreneurs in my research were mothers. According to the London Development Agency (LDA, 2005), increasing numbers of women are using self-employment as a way to juggle family commitments and childcare while harnessing their earning potential. They are part of a new breed of alternative entrepreneurs – 'alterpreneurs' – seeking to create a more suitable work/life balance tailored to meet their own specific needs. Rather than aspiring to grow large businesses for the sake of enterprise and vast wealth, they are keen to start up small businesses to avoid the 'corporate treadmill' of traditional employment (Critical 2 Limited, 2005).

Elaine had enjoyed a successful career working for local government and development organizations when she decided to take the plunge and become a freelance consultant. Motivated in part by her disillusionment with her employers, her decision was also largely fuelled by the demands of trying to balance a career with her primary responsibility for childcare. Elaine described her transition to self-employment positively:

I've given up working full time. I'm self-employed now [and] the work situation has made quite a big difference in the home life, because now I'm spending much more time with my children than I was before ... I was a Principal Consultant [but left] for a number of reasons, including that the work ... always seemed to be somewhere [far] from here. So I guess that's one of the things that I didn't enjoy about it. But I did enjoy the experience of acting as a consultant. So initially I just planned to hand my notice in and then I spoke to somebody that happened to be my line manager at the time and they said, 'Why don't you register with us and go freelance, just do it as your own business. We'd still use you ... We've got a good working relationship with you.' ... So that's what I did ... So, I do more or less the same work – consultancy for local government. I get some work through [my previous employers] and some through word of mouth. I haven't actually done lots of canvassing and marketing, most of the work has just come in through knowing people ... And that's working really well. I don't have loads and loads of work, but I have enough work to keep me busy, so that I can still have time with the children and do stuff around the house and that. So it's just a much more leisurely lifestyle. And I suppose the thing I always thought would be difficult would be money and actually I haven't noticed it at all ... Probably I've earned [the same] but have only done about four months' work for a year. But I suppose I wouldn't have been able to do it if I didn't have a husband [with] a secure income, because obviously you've got to pay the mortgage every month, you've got to pay your childcare fees every month. Whereas I didn't have any money at all until probably December and then I got £30,000 all at the same time. But it's quite liberating. And now I think why don't [more] people do it?

(Elaine, consultant)

She elaborated on her liking of self-employment and explained that the additional freedom and flexibility it gave her contrasted sharply with her previous lifestyle of never feeling she had enough time for her family:

Spending time with the children was a motivation as well. It's just like, why do you have children and then spend all your time sending them to nursery and just rushing them around? Rushing them to get to school, rushing them to have a bath, rushing them to have their tea, rushing them to bed, haven't got time to read a book to them ... and I know that in comparison to a lot of people the work style that I had was really flexible anyway. But the difference is just amazing ... you can say to people, 'Yeah I can do that contract, but I'm not working that week, because it's half term' and nobody will bat an eyelid ... Would they be like that to their own employees? They wouldn't.

(Elaine, consultant)

Despite having lots of work in the first year of business, Elaine and her family relocated overseas and she experienced a period of much reduced activity for her business. In a subsequent interview she commented:

> I haven't done any work since November, which I'm sure I should feel bad about but I don't … and then part of me thinks, 'Well, it's just as well that I haven't had any work, because [my husband]'s had work permanently and it's just been nice to be able to be with the kids.'

> (Elaine, consultant)

Although Elaine and her husband both did freelance consultancy, her particular skills commanded a higher rate of pay. Nevertheless, she remained the primary carer for their children and continued to do most of the household chores. Minoritized women who are married and entrepreneurs frequently face difficulties juggling the demands of their business with having the main responsibility for childcare and the home, and are generally dependent on informal support networks for coping (Omar *et al.*, 2004). Even so, they find self-employment worthwhile because of the flexibility. These gendered difficulties contrast with the situation in Sweden, where female entrepreneurialism is flourishing and provision of childcare is a government priority. Notably, when research was carried out with women in Sweden, 'childcare was not once mentioned as a barrier to starting an enterprise, whereas in the UK it is one of the most frequently cited obstacles' (Prowess, 2005: 16).

Elaine reflected that conforming to traditional gender roles within the home had in many ways proved more rewarding than the exhausting reality of juggling career and family as a professional woman:

> At the end of the day, maybe you should just conform to the roles. Maybe it's just a lot less stressful, 'cause now, I guess I do conform to the role. I do the cleaning, the cooking and stuff. I don't do no outside work 'cause that's man's job … and the house runs a lot nicer. And it's like, 'Don't talk to me about finance.' That's another thing, I've stopped being worried about it. It's like [my husband says], 'We haven't got enough money,' [and I say] 'Oh yeah, what do you want for dinner?'

> (Elaine, consultant)

Although she spoke tongue in cheek, it is true that the demands of career and family can prove a heavy burden for professional women. Arguably, the media and society sell women an unrealistic dream of 'having it all' and the education system does not teach teenage girls studying for A levels anything to prepare them for juggling career, partner and children (Channel 4 Television, 2006). Yet, this was a key issue that every mother in my research struggled to deal with.

Interestingly, although most participants had entrepreneurial leanings, few thought it important to work for oneself per se. Their entrepreneurial endeavours served primarily as a means to an end. Participants described freedom, autonomy and financial security as key benefits of working for themselves, which concurs with Barclays' (2005) findings. However, Barclays (2005) overlooked the dynamics of racism in its research and the reality is that many minoritized women have to create their own jobs if they wish to do work commensurate with their qualifications and experience (Maurey, 2005).

This brings me to my third cluster of entrepreneurs, who were attracted to entrepreneurialism when they saw their careers plateau at an early stage. Unlike other minoritized entrepreneurs, the most common reason cited by black respondents for starting their own business is to make better use of their skills (CI Research, 2006). My research corroborated this, in that self-employed participants felt that their skills, rather than their race, determined their business success:

> Working for myself I don't think [race has] had an impact at all. I think if anything people were surprised in the earlier days when I came knocking on the door ... when they were expecting somebody to arrive at their door to do this whiz bang presentation. I could see in some of their faces, 'What, it's you! You're going to do this for us!' ... You can just tell that people were surprised. And I'm a person that [believes], 'At the end of the day, I'm not here to prove myself to you. I know what I can do. If you want it, you want it. If you've got a problem, then that's your problem, not mine.'
>
> (Zac, entrepreneur)

Minoritized entrepreneurs rarely experience overt discrimination in business (Barclays, 2005) and my research illustrates that it is the discrimination in employment, rather than in business, that is the problem. This makes some minoritized people want to set up their own enterprises (Wingfield, 2011). The obstacles faced by these participants to their career progression within their organizations were associated with interpersonal dynamics rather than with their skills. Self-employment enabled a shift of emphasis, from fitting in with colleagues to being able to do the job well.

In spite of his qualifications, experience and community endeavours, such as being a magistrate and school governor, Neil's desired career progression remained elusive. He began to explore the prospect of self-employment as a life coach. He confessed that he was not particularly inclined to entrepreneurialism, but his ongoing frustration had driven him to consider self-employment.

After Sean's first business folded, he returned to adult education and after graduating he secured employment with a local authority. But when his employers privatized he faced job insecurity in a less regulated environment of office politics and racial dynamics. He explained his reasons for wanting to return to self-employment:

> I could actually be nurturing the potential and trying to progress within the field I'm in, but I don't feel that's the direction for me, because I can see a lot of the barriers. There's still racial barriers [and] a lot of stereotypes. There's still a lot of favouritism going on within the organization ... So, yes education helps, but there are still a lot of [biases] within a particular organization. So, I don't see it as the way forward. I see the way forward is starting your own business and being fair within your own organization and having total control really.
>
> (Sean, housing advice manager)

In the UK, black professionals 'frequently encounter identity-challenging situations as they interact with explicit and implicit models of race and stereotyping' (Atewologun and Singh, 2010: 332). In response to his career frustrations and persistent desire to work for himself, Sean began incubating two business ventures. The first was intended as a launch pad to generate more capital that would enable him to start up his second idea, which was more community oriented and much closer to his heart.

In *The Black Middle Classes* (BBC Radio 4, 2006), Mike Phillips predicted that people setting up their own businesses in response to constraints within the mainstream would be central to the development of a more prosperous segment among black communities in the UK. However, poor access to funding is a major barrier (DTI, 2003; Maurey, 2005): the multiplier effect of race, class and gender bias takes its toll. For instance, when regeneration funding is available, it is more likely to go to applicants from middle-class areas who propose developing businesses within deprived areas, rather than to applicants from the regeneration area itself (Dawe *et al.*, 2006). This has implications for minoritized people, who are often concentrated in these traditionally poor communities. Uneven distribution across ethnicities also leaves minoritized people at a disadvantage (LDA, 2005). In my cohort, Sean was not alone in finding this a problem for his first business and a stumbling block for his subsequent ideas.

When financing new businesses, women are more likely to require loans for business start-ups than men, who tend to have access to savings (Dawe *et al.*, 2006). Targeted funding for minoritized women's business start-ups (DTI, 2003) and directing proportionate funding towards minoritized business owners (LDA, 2005: 9) could tackle this issue effectively and initiate real change.

Another stumbling block is the need for appropriate business mentors (Nelson, 2004). Each young entrepreneur – Eve, Zac and Sean – highlighted their lack of a business mentor when they started up their business. Having more business mentors with whom black entrepreneurs could identify would help them to avoid some of the common pitfalls that fledgling businesses encounter and to develop their business management skills.

Entrepreneurial spirit, intertwined with community orientation for many of the graduates in my research, and their commitment to their communities influenced their careers.

## Community orientation in careers

Community-building is common among minoritized women (Maurey, 2005) and black women professionals frequently negotiate careers and community commitment (Gilkes, 1982). Young African-Caribbean women often desire to improve conditions for black communities, working in caring professions such as teaching, social work and nursing (Mirza, 1992). Volunteering in the community is also common among mature, working-class Access students (Reay, 2003).

My research identified that participants had a desire to improve conditions for black communities by providing services to meet their needs, or by 'giving back' in some way. This dimension of their career aspirations was often aligned to their entrepreneurial ideas. Most of the participants had not geared their businesses specifically to niche African-Caribbean markets, but an aspiration to combine entrepreneurialism with serving community needs surfaced in the interviews.

Dean had business ideas related to community development, such as providing holistic therapy services for older people, mentoring black youths and creating an organization that worked closely with schools to ensure accountability to members of the black community. Dean had an understanding of how to access government funding for such projects, but believed that ventures should be under the control and ownership of the black community, not a local authority. He explained that projects had folded in the past when funders changed their priorities, but community ownership would ensure that the projects could continue.

Sean also described a community-oriented idea that would utilize his existing skills base and help to improve conditions for African-Caribbean communities. He described a one-stop website tailored to support and empower people in challenging unfair systems in public sector services.

The career choices of Eve, Nora and Michelle also reflected community spirit. They saw added value in working in schools with diverse student bodies and large numbers of black and African-Caribbean pupils. They believed that, as black teachers, they helped to improve black pupils' school experiences and, at the same time, they felt appreciated. Michelle chose to move from a popular, well-resourced private school to work in a less successful but more diverse state school, because of the race and class dynamics within these environments. Regarding the private school she said:

> [Posh High] wasn't working, because ... I didn't really suit that environment very well ... and although I was one of the most qualified there – so it wasn't that I was out of my league educationally – culturally I was not welcome there ... It was very middle class, very white, the parents were paying. I could tell that quite a few parents weren't very pleased when they turned up to parents' evening and I was there with my locks and my brown face and they didn't want to shake your hands.
>
> (Michelle, teacher)

But she felt appreciated and welcome in her next school, where resources were more limited but the student population far more diverse and multicultural. She was also happy to have secured a full-time contract:

> I'm pleased, because I feel that that is a little bit of a success, because I'm the only [temporary staff] that they've kept. They haven't got the money, but they've still kept me anyway. And I am enjoying the work there, not just the teaching but the interaction with the children and the other staff ... It's in Lambeth so a lot of the children are black, but because it's in Clapham you've also got a lot of middle-class white children, so there's a real mixture ... and at the moment I'd say the predominant culture in the school is black.
>
> (Michelle, teacher)

By forfeiting opportunities to work in prestigious institutions, these participants were able to give something back to black communities and simultaneously avoid feeling isolated in their work. Reay (2003) notes that community commitment of this kind can affect women's financial return on investment in higher education. However, for some professional black women 'success is defined in terms of community achievements and positive evaluation by colleagues, rather than material rewards' (Gilkes, 1982: 289).

Voluntary endeavours were another way to serve black communities, and several participants saw their involvement in my research project as a way to improve conditions for black communities. By telling their stories they could highlight for others the issues they had faced in their education and careers, and at the same time encourage black children. Zac reflected on his own early days as a pupil attending a special school:

> I'm getting to a stage where I feel that I've got to give something back. I haven't reached that stage yet, but I do feel I want to give something back. Whether that's mentoring younger black boys or adopting a boy or whatever ... whether it's a young 16-year-old, just saying, 'Look, you can do this. These things are there.' Because the kids, especially black boys, they need to see that ... you don't have to be a footballer, a pop star, in sport to make money. As a black person you can do all these other things and you can start ... from going to a special school and getting your sweets and stars and stuff.
>
> (Zac, entrepreneur)

Zac followed his aspiration through, later becoming a business and entrepreneurship mentor; and Michelle demonstrated her commitment to community development by starting a supplementary Saturday school. She explained her rationale:

> [I run a] Saturday school ... I've got ten children that come regularly ... I'm having to teach the children Maths and Science and History ... It was mainly to help black children, but not just for black children [and] I just wanted them to understand a little bit about Africa and the Caribbean. And give them a flavour of that, because our schools ... the way they teach is Eurocentric. But the damaging thing [is] if your ancestry is not in Europe you begin to feel that your group hasn't contributed to anything and you're almost fortunate to be here in Europe. But that is very much a power and control thing ... In order for you to be able

to contribute to any society that you're in, you need to have ... confidence in your own self and in what your people have done. So you come back with something positive. So that's why I'm teaching them an African language. Not because I expect them to be fluent in it.

(Michelle, teacher)

The graduates' community orientation, combined with their entrepreneurial spirit, suggests that linking small business and community development initiatives to the growing numbers of minoritized and black graduates could help regenerate communities in the UK and thus promote economic and social inclusion.

## Conclusions

The extent to which participants felt that their present careers and career prospects were commensurate with their academic achievements indicated the extrinsic value of education for black graduates. Graduation enhanced the career prospects of all, enabling them to embark upon a professional career, which a few found extremely rewarding. However, most paid an ethnic penalty, which reduced the value of their degrees, curtailing the return on their investment in higher education.

We saw the respondents' predisposition towards public sector careers, entrepreneurialism and community service. Public sector careers, and in particular teaching, were popular. A clearly defined career route and funding for teacher training, combined with the emphasis on equal opportunities in public sector recruitment, meant that they were able to secure employment as graduates. However, many remained at the lower levels of their professions far longer than they anticipated, and disputes and conflict punctuated their careers. These issues were frequently viewed as arising from covert racism and being an outsider.

There was a strong entrepreneurial spirit among the participants, in some cases augmented by lack of career progress as employees. Entrepreneurial endeavours allowed them to bypass organizational constraints and utilize their existing skills to their own advantage. Most had been self-employed at some point during their careers, but accessing funding was a recurring problem.

We saw a race dynamic and a gender dynamic to both teaching careers and entrepreneurialism. Teaching enabled mothers to work similar hours to their children's school time while self-employment allowed the flexibility to manage work and family commitments better. However, the conflicting demands of paid work and childcare had negative consequences for the mothers and sustaining a balance was an ongoing challenge.

Several participants demonstrated a community orientation which manifested in business ideas that contained a community-building dimension, voluntary work and career choices that provided an opportunity to 'put back' into black communities.

The participants in this research represent part of a growing pool of professional African-Caribbean workers in Britain who are achieving in the face of societal structures that limit their options. On the one hand, the inequalities faced by many in the workplace have led to a waste of their talents and ability. On the other hand, their inclination towards entrepreneurial and community endeavours represents an opportunity to harness that potential and redirect it towards enhancing black communities. Investment in black graduates such as these would help build more vibrant communities and a stronger UK economy.

## Chapter 6
# Conclusions

> In a racist society for a black child to become educated is to contradict the whole system of racist signification ... to succeed in studying white knowledge is to undo the system itself ... to refute its reproduction of black inferiority materially and symbolically.
>
> (Casey, 1993: 123)

## Introduction

This concluding chapter draws together my main findings. Reproduction theory, critical race theory, black feminism and intersectionality provided the theoretical framework for the research. I draw on the literature that explores the stages of black students' education – compulsory schooling, post-compulsory education and higher education – and also on the literature about the careers of minoritized and women professionals.

I have sought to present the full journey of the research participants, through their education and into their careers, to cast light on how black learners interact with societal structures and institutions to achieve educational success. It also brings into focus the extrinsic value of education for black graduates, by considering the extent to which participants felt that their careers and career prospects were commensurate with their qualifications.

Through my qualitative research approach, I sought insight into the educational experiences of ten black graduates. All were born in the UK of African-Caribbean parents and educated entirely within the British educational system. It is their perspectives that I represent, treating them as knowing subjects. Their own perceptions of their own educational journeys and resultant career outcomes are presented through their responses to my research questions:

- How do black graduates experience the structures of race, class and gender in employment and educational settings?
- What resources do black graduates draw upon to navigate these domains and enable their successes?

- In what ways do black graduates consider it important to use their skills and experiences to challenge the inequalities of race, class and gender in British society?

The first three sections of this chapter summarize the answers to the research questions. In the fourth section I outline the policy implications and further research directions, and summarize the key findings.

## Experiencing the structures of race, class and gender

In this section I outline the structural trajectory of participants across the domains of compulsory education, post-compulsory education and career, and reveal some of the common experiences of the structuring effects of race, class and gender for black graduates.

Both race and social class had a detrimental impact on the research participants' access to effective schooling. Gender dynamics added another layer of complexity.

Government policy identifies the benchmark of school success as five GCSE passes at grades A* to C, including English Language and Maths (EHRC, 2011). Eight of the ten graduate participants did not achieve this by the end of their compulsory schooling, which is a disturbing statistic evident also in the literature. DfES (2003) reported that the performance of African-Caribbean pupils is often better than that of their counterparts from other ethnicities when they start school, but declines as they progress through the education system until they end up as one of the lowest-achieving ethnic groups at school leaving age. This pattern is evident among the research cohort, many of whom started off well but acquired little by way of school leaving qualifications. Narratives were littered with references to unfulfilled potential and negative experiences, especially in secondary school.

Working-class children in poorly resourced inner city schools are less likely to enjoy educational success than their middle-class counterparts and the link between socio-economic class and academic achievement persists (Hutchinson *et al.*, 2011). The history of colonialism and post-war mass immigration from the former British colonies positioned first-generation African-Caribbean migrants firmly among the British working class in terms of their access to jobs, housing and education (Coard, 1971). The situation for the twenty-first century is much the same. Black children are largely concentrated in inner city schools (Rhamie and Hallam, 2002) and my research participants were no exception. Few of their parents were educated to graduate level or in professional occupations and all my participants attended non-selective, state secondary schools, where several felt that insufficient attention was paid to securing academic achievement.

However, for black children issues of class and race are complex (Education Commission, 2004) and the correlation between social class and educational attainment is less obvious among black pupils than white (DfES, 2003). Furthermore, gender dynamics alter the experiences of girls and boys. On the one hand, black boys from middle-class backgrounds tend to achieve less than their working-class counterparts from other ethnicities (Education Commission, 2004). On the other hand, black girls tend to achieve more than their white counterparts from similar socio-economic circumstances (Mirza, 2005).

The most fundamental issue that emerged in discussions was the impact of poor teacher–student relationships, which were fraught with difficulties and underpinned by negative racial stereotyping. Boys felt that conflict with teachers affected their education. They were given significant encouragement for sports, but little for academic work. The self-fulfilling prophecy of academic failure ensued and four of the five boys left school with no good GCSE equivalents. The girls were most affected by low teacher expectations and they found themselves streamed into lower-ability groups and given poor careers advice. Ironically, the role of teachers in hindering the girls' progress was more obvious because there was no outright conflict. Instead, there was a dumbing down of the girls' expectations, which limited their opportunities. Four of the five girls left school with only two or three good GCSE equivalents.

Parental involvement in the learning process is considered one of the most important elements of school success (Desforges and Abouchaar, 2003) and a key problem faced by many black children is the inability of their parents to secure a good education for them and challenge any unfair treatment (McKenley, 2005). Working-class parents tend to see education as something that happens only at school (Evans, 2006) and many African-Caribbean parents retain a blind faith in the system (Coard, 1971). This was true for most participants, who felt that their parents had a hands-off approach to education, despite having high expectations and strong family discourses of education being the key to success. Parents were often reluctant to challenge teachers' authority and, in the most extreme case, one participant had been expelled. School experiences, it transpired, were largely about learning to fail. But this began to change as my participants progressed into post-compulsory education.

Eight of the ten participants followed non-traditional routes into higher education so their progression was slower than the traditional trajectory for middle-class students. Only two interviewees followed the traditional path, successfully completing GCSE equivalents at 16, A levels at 18 and then continuing directly to higher education.

Once they had made the decision to study in higher education, participants' main obstacle was financial, as they sacrificed their earning potential in order to study. This class-related issue was accentuated for the mature students, who had more responsibilities than the typical young student. The accumulation of debt and the competing demands of working while studying presented significant problems for some participants. Although successive governments over recent decades have declared their commitment to widening participation in higher education and improving opportunities for social mobility, the removal of student grants and the increasing tuition fees say otherwise. The greater financial burden on the majority of students is particularly damaging – or discouraging – to those from less affluent backgrounds.

Nonetheless, my participants progressed into higher education, where they perfected the art of learning to achieve in an educational setting. They described their experiences of higher education as far more worthwhile and positive than school. They enjoyed widening horizons and the cultural capital of improved confidence in their own ability. However, they were mindful of the race and gender inequity in higher education and the intersection of class dynamics. They explored the impact that the lack of diversity in staffing and curriculum in higher education had on them as minoritized students.

At school, participants encountered problems in their relationships with teachers which affected their school outcomes. At university, however, their relationships with lecturers were quite different. Participants were less dependent on good teacher–student relationships and this was central to their success. Relationships with lecturers were generally distant, which reduced the potential for antagonism, but held disadvantages of its own. For instance, some participants perceived that they and other black students had less supportive relationships with their lecturers than their white counterparts did.

Some graduates in my study experienced subtle, offensive put-downs that conveyed low expectations and racist attitudes from staff in their higher education institutions. Microaggressions are often unintentional, but they are damaging nonetheless and so need to be challenged (Solórzano, 1998). However, those participants did not think complaining was a viable option. The power dynamics of teacher–student relationships and the lack of institutional awareness and support for tackling covert racism ensured that they suffered in silence. Instead, they adopted coping strategies, distancing themselves from the staff in question and withdrawing expectations of support. Reynolds (2006) and Rodgers (2006) both assert that many black students do not access the support available in higher education. My research corroborates this and goes further, recognizing this behaviour as emotional withdrawal used by these students as a defence mechanism – as a shrewd response to the onslaught of microaggressions and the unfavourable treatment they encountered in education.

Black academic staff in higher education are still under-represented (HESA, 1998, 2008, 2011) and this exacerbates the alienation of black students and starves them of support from significant others, who might understand and be in a position to help with the problems they encounter with racism. Black academics are concentrated in the lower levels of the profession (ECU, 2014), so they are not in a position to influence policy significantly. It is little surprise, then, that strategies for tackling racism are not a priority in higher education institutions. My participants were unanimous in calling for more black staff at various levels in higher education institutions. Nonetheless the statistics (e.g. ECU, 2014) suggest that discrimination continues to be an issue in the recruitment and career progression of black academics.

This lack of diversity in staffing is echoed in the lack of diversity in the curriculum. Virtually all my respondents criticized the curriculum on their courses for failing to reflect the racial diversity of the UK or of the world. In these times of unprecedented emphasis on globalization and internationalism, it is ironic that a truly diverse curriculum has yet to materialize in British universities. The paucity of black culture, literature, art, history, or scientists and scientific knowledge reproduces and reinforces a racist, Eurocentric epistemology at a subliminal level. The ignoring or concealing of black contributions to civilization sends a clear message to students that they are of no account. In particular, teacher training courses were strongly criticized for failing to prepare future teachers for a diverse school population. This perpetuates the problem of poor teacher–student relationships and the consequences for black children.

Some black students counter the Eurocentric bias of the mainstream higher education curriculum by pursuing a knowledge of their own histories and heroes outside higher education (Allen, P., 1998). But, hooks (1994) suggests that black and working-class students should challenge the dominance of white, middle-class values from within higher education, by persistently injecting their own perspectives and not acquiescing to the existing norms. I explored this idea with my interviewees and found that some were creative in bringing a black perspective to their studies where possible. However, they recognized that this was risky as they were acutely aware that it made some lecturers feel uncomfortable. Interviewees who wrote about race from a black perspective felt that they were penalized with markedly lower grades so they became apprehensive about the cost of expressing a black viewpoint. Where grades and relationships with lecturers are at risk, students who lack confidence in their abilities, and particularly those who enter higher education via a non-traditional route, can lack the cultural capital needed to stand up to staff. It can be extremely difficult to challenge the institutional norms from an already disadvantaged position. This is one more example of microaggressions and the ways that those in power subtly silence black voices within the higher education context.

Many of my interviewees entered higher education as mature students and were anxious about being isolated and not fitting in. Before going to university, they harboured the idea that university was not for people like them so they anticipated not fitting in on the grounds of age, class and race. Reay (2002) identifies class difference as at the root of working-class students' fear. For many of my research participants, ethnicity compounded this and ultimately manifested in a reluctance to reveal any cultural traits and in believing they were unable to be 'real' at university.

We saw that some of the students were fearful of failing. Reay (2001) and Reynolds (2006) found that higher education students who have had negative experiences of school can experience feelings of inadequacy and anxiety about their academic ability. Many of my participants doubted their own ability before they started university and feared that they would fail to meet the standards required. The sense of inadequacy conveyed by some of them suggested that their understanding of the interconnection between family background and educational attainment was so deeply rooted that they doubted the evidence of their own academic achievements. Yet, in reality, they proved to be perfectly capable of meeting the standards and most went on to study at postgraduate level.

Analysis of the professional lives of black men and women in the UK is relatively undocumented. Most of the relevant literature has focused on the experiences of the broader category of minoritized professionals or the narrower category of black women. Examining the extent to which participants felt that their present careers and career prospects were commensurate with their academic achievements raised the issue of the extrinsic value of education for black graduates. My findings suggest that an 'ethnic penalty' (Modood *et al.*, 1997) continues to reduce the value of a degree for most participants, curtailing the financial and professional return on investment in higher education.

There are growing numbers of minoritized graduates in the UK, yet unemployment rates remain 'significantly higher for people from every ethnic minority when compared with White people' (EHRC, 2015: 37). Black employees have experienced the biggest drop in pay rates in recent years and black graduates earn 23 per cent less than their white counterparts (TUC, 2016). Alarmingly, the more qualified the black employee is, the bigger the pay gap between them and similarly qualified white workers (TUC, 2016).

Girls and women outperform their male equivalents in education, but continue to earn less than men. They are concentrated in part-time work and lower-paid employment sectors (EHRC, 2015). There is also 'a lack of diversity in senior and managerial occupations (in terms of gender and ethnicity) ... and at board level in both the public and private sector' (EHRC, 2015: 99).

Minoritized workers are concentrated in some sectors of the job market and rarely found in others. Many black women find work in the public sector, where suitably qualified minoritized people can gain entry because of the priority given to equal opportunities in recruitment. In her seminal research, Mirza (1992) identified that black women selected 'strategic careers', taking into account race and gender stratification within the UK employment market. I would add that public sector employment has the reputation of being lower paid but more secure than private sector employment. This job security can be a big incentive for qualified people who experience marginalization within the workforce. However, government austerity measures in recent years have diminished that security significantly. Public sector job cuts have mostly affected women (McKay *et al.*, 2013) and the rise in insecure, low-paid and part-time work has had its biggest impact on minoritized workers (TUC, 2015a). Black women are at the intersection of both.

Not one interviewee in my research was employed by a private sector organization. Nine had public sector careers, mostly in teaching. Most participants did not set out with a teaching career in mind, but the availability of funding for PGCEs and the structured, direct route into professional employment in a relatively short time made it an attractive and accessible career choice. It thus emerged as a default career. The teaching profession also proved attractive for the mothers in the research, who were all the primary carers of their children. As growing numbers of women enter the employment market, there has been no corresponding decrease in their roles as primary carers within the family (Hughes, 2002; Omar *et al.*, 2004). Accordingly, mothers increasingly struggle with the competing pressures of family commitments and career (Hughes, 2002). This tension was evident among my participants and teaching allowed an easier fit with childcare commitments than most careers.

The large number of women and the growing number of minoritized people in the teaching profession are rarely at the top of the organizational hierarchy, which remains largely the preserve of white men. And in spite of teaching initially providing a safe haven for the participants to utilize their skills in professional employment, all but one became cynical about their teaching career. The glass ceiling hinders the career progression of large numbers of women, who encounter a gender penalty. Nelson's (2004) 'sticky floor syndrome' describes the situation where minoritized women remain at the bottom of their professions due to the intersection of gender and race discrimination. But it is not only women who face discrimination in their career paths on the grounds of race and Modood *et al.* (1997) call this an 'ethnic penalty'.

Most participants who were employed, rather than self-employed, remained at the lower levels of their professions. Career frustrations were punctuated by official and unofficial disputes and conflict. Participants gave examples of line managers actively seeking information to discredit them and of other, less qualified and less experienced, white colleagues bypassing them in career progression. Consequently, at the end of the primary research, only one of the eight interviewees who was employed, rather than self-employed, had maintained a senior position. Despite several years in employment, the majority of the group were frustrated that their careers seemed to have plateaued at an early stage.

The participants generally perceived that their negative experiences in organizations were due to covert racism or being an outsider. In a racialized context where few black employees secure professional or senior positions, many face isolation in their careers and detachment from their communities (hooks, 1993). The literature on bicultural lifestyles (Gordon, 2007) explores the ways in which black professionals juggle the demands of predominantly white, middle-class, male-oriented organizational cultures when their own backgrounds are embedded in the norms of disenfranchised black communities. Gordon (2007) stresses the need for black workers to attend vigilantly to internal conflicts that arise from this duality. On the one hand, not fitting into the old boys' network had a detrimental impact on some participants' career progression. On the other hand, being the only black person in a senior position added pressure to succeed on behalf of their race. So what resources did they draw on?

## Resources for succeeding

This book is concerned with how black graduates succeed in the education system and their careers, despite the structural disadvantages they face. The second research question explored the strategies the participants used to navigate success within the domains of school, post-compulsory education and careers.

Their compulsory education was largely a story of unfulfilled potential, but a few positive influences in their school experiences were identified. Black teachers, for example, helped to reduce the unfair treatment participants encountered. From within the system, black and anti-racist teachers can mitigate the soul-destroying impact of racism. This emphasizes the importance of improving diversity in schools via proactive measures such as recruiting more black staff and training all teachers on the issues relating to race, racism and diversity. Similarly, the need to develop a diverse curriculum in compulsory education cannot be over-emphasized. In addition to this, the parents of African-Caribbean children need to be able to support their children in school and so it should be incumbent upon schools, as government-sanctioned education providers, to facilitate their positive engagement by encouraging genuine collaboration and open dialogue.

During school, about half of my research participants had their sights set on higher education. Their paths to higher education were direct, but somewhat protracted, involving a series of stepping stones needed to compensate for insufficient school leaving qualifications. The other half of the group did not consider university an option while they were at school and their paths to higher education were serendipitous. They were spurred on to continue in education by a transition of some sort, usually including a dramatic change of circumstances, or encouragement from significant others who redirected them towards higher education by assisting with careers or academic advice. Some significant others were peers who had studied in university themselves, so presented it as an achievable objective. Others were people in positions of authority who believed in the research participants' capabilities.

Notably, in all but one case, the significant others were black, or actively involved in improving conditions for black communities. This theme recurred in higher education where, in the rare instances that participants had a particularly supportive relationship with a member of the teaching staff, it was with someone from a minoritized background. Clearly, the attitude to race of the supportive person is instrumental in their enabling these black students to transcend racial barriers. And it appears that students are more receptive to the positive influence of supporters who can identify with their race or ethnicity. Having minoritized and anti-racist staff in key positions in higher education, who can support and encourage black students, is therefore of the utmost importance.

People from all backgrounds choose to enter higher education for similar reasons, but the disadvantaged position of minoritized people in the employment market makes it more imperative for them to acquire qualifications (Allen, A., 1998). All my interviewees saw education as the key to success and believed that a degree would improve their life chances. The strongest motivation to pursue higher education was social mobility, expressed as 'widening life choices', 'increasing earning potential' and 'improving career prospects'. Most of my participants were hoping to achieve financial security and were less concerned about their social class status.

Whereas teachers and friends are more influential for white students, family expectations tend to be more important for minoritized students (Allen, A., 1998). The majority of my respondents indicated that family expectations stimulated their progression to further education, but in most cases they were not expected to go to higher education. The women in my research tended to perceive family expectations as support and encouragement for their own decision to study, but the men were much more inclined to perceive family expectations as pressure. Their school teachers' expectations were insignificant and their success was in spite of the teachers' low assessment of their ability.

Although the literature states that minoritized students are less motivated by enjoying learning, my research found that 'pleasure of studying' was one of the most important motivating factors, particularly for the women. Several relished the learning experience and described a deeply felt desire to learn, which seemed to stem from the soul. Moore (1992) defines the soul as the central place deep within us, the core of our being and the very essence of who we are. It is the place from which the deepest of emotions, inner drives and motivations come and where true satisfaction and contentment are experienced. Like a compass, the soul can guide us through our lives and this seemed to be the case for those participants who gained great pleasure from learning. These participants sustained their studies to master's degree level. Arguably, pleasure in learning is key in motivating black participation in higher education.

Black support networks are also an important resource for black students. Many develop informal black support networks, both consciously and unconsciously, to insulate themselves against racism and isolation (Allen, P., 1998). For example, the African-Caribbean men in Reynolds (2006) used strong peer networks of black and mature students to alleviate their internal struggle between university life and real life. For most of my interviewees, African-Caribbean Societies or other black support networks were central to their university lives. They were acutely aware of the small number of black students within their higher education institutions and so valued the opportunity to associate with students they identified with, which gave them a much needed sense of belonging.

In the UK, black and minoritized students are concentrated in new universities and in London. Ball *et al.* (2002) suggest that when it comes to choosing higher education institutions, social class has more influence than ethnicity among minoritized students. However, my interviewees considered a range of race and class dynamics when choosing their higher education institution. Most studied at post-1992 universities and, as the literature suggests (Taylor, 1992; Allen, A., 1998), preferred institutions that were close to family or in ethnically diverse locations. They utilized their unique African-Caribbean social capital, as opposed to middle-class social capital, by tapping into black social networks such as family, church and African-Caribbean Societies. Whereas white middle-class students use middle-class social capital to choose prestigious higher education institutions, my students used their African-Caribbean social capital to create a sense of security and support while studying in higher education and to obviate the risk of not fitting in because of their race and class. If students feel alienated they may well drop out. The potential downside is that students self-select out of prestigious institutions and the associated cultural capital that could enhance their career prospects. It is an indictment of traditional universities that so many black students feel that they have to choose between belonging and prestige.

Being outside the right social networks for career progression hindered a number of those who were employees and consequently they perceived entrepreneurialism as a way to manage their career progression independently. Self-employment in the UK has expanded (Purcell, 2000) and is a new direction taken by increasing numbers of black workers and women (Nelson, 2004; Maurey, 2005; Wingfield, 2011). Encouraging business start-ups among women could provide a route out of poverty for many (Nelson, 2004) and minoritized enterprises could promote economic inclusion as a generator of social and financial capital (Barclays, 2005).

Eight of the ten interviewees had been fully or partially self-employed at some time and followed one of three paths to self-employment. The first cluster were young entrepreneurs who launched their first businesses in their twenties, after just a few years of working in their chosen fields. The second group were mothers seeking to balance career and family commitments. The third group were attracted to entrepreneurialism when they saw their careers plateau at an early stage.

Self-employed participants in my research described freedom, autonomy and financial security as the key benefits of working for themselves. Their narratives also suggested that entrepreneurialism enabled them to circumvent elements of sexism and racism they experienced in traditional employment. In terms of gender, self-employment provided mothers with much-needed flexibility to manage their caring commitments more effectively alongside their careers. In terms of race, self-employment shifted the emphasis from fitting in with colleagues in order to achieve career progression, to having the ability to fulfil the requirements of the job. As entrepreneurs, they perceived that their skills, rather than their race, determined their success.

## Challenging the structures of race, class and gender

Here I answer the third research question, exploring the ways participants sought to use their skills and experiences to challenge the structures of race, class and gender at a community level. This offers important insights and understanding of the connections for African-Caribbean graduates between education and community service.

Freire (1996) and hooks (1994) argue that education should achieve 'conscientization', which is social and political transformation. This theme was most apparent in relation to careers, where my participants sought to challenge the structuring effects of race and class by channelling the cultural capital they had gained through education to serve their community. Most spoke about wanting to enhance the opportunities of future generations of African-Caribbean people in Britain. This demonstrates their conscientization in their growing understanding of how the structures of society shape our lives and how they, as individuals, could effect change.

Community-building endeavours are a common factor among minoritized women (Maurey, 2005) and many black women professionals intertwine their careers with community commitment (Gilkes, 1982). Mirza's research (1992) on the career aspirations of young African-Caribbean women found that they wished to improve conditions for black communities by working in caring professions such as teaching, social work and nursing. Similarly, Reay (2003) identifies volunteering in the community as a common theme and a strong motivator among her mature, working-class Access students.

The desire of my participants to improve conditions for black communities by providing services to meet their needs or 'giving back' in some way was often aligned to their entrepreneurial ideas. Most of those who had been self-employed during their careers had not specifically geared their businesses to niche black or African-Caribbean markets but aspired to combine entrepreneurialism with serving the community. The career choices of some of the teachers reflected the same community spirit. They valued the opportunity to work in schools with large numbers of minoritized and black students, because in these contexts they were able to improve the school experiences of black pupils and they also felt that their contributions were appreciated. Forfeiting opportunities to work in more prestigious institutions allowed them to give back to black communities, which made their work more meaningful and worthwhile. At the same time, they felt less isolated within their profession. Reay (2003) notes that community commitment of this kind can affect women's financial return on investment in higher education study by reducing their earning potential. However, for some professional black women 'success is defined in terms of community achievements and positive evaluation by colleagues, rather than material rewards (Gilkes, 1982: 289).

Voluntary work was another element of community involvement that enabled participants to encourage black children towards careers beyond the sports and music presented by the media as the domain of black professionals. Participants were involved in supplementary Saturday schools and mentoring, which are black community-driven initiatives designed to tackle the problems faced by black children in education.

My respondents were as sensitive to gender inequality in higher education as they were to race inequality. Most believed that there was a need for more female staff at various levels of academia and a feminist perspective throughout the core curriculum. Women are over-represented as students in higher education, yet under-represented as academic staff, particularly at the top of the academic ladder (ECU, 2014). In my research, postgraduate study was more prevalent among the women participants than the men and their love of study was a much stronger motivation. Four of the five women acquired teaching qualifications and master's degrees and three of those considered undertaking PhD research.

The women who expressed interest in studying for a PhD all wanted to research issues pertinent to black communities. This is an interesting revelation relating to the conscientization of black graduates and their potential to change things in the world. But here the class dynamic re-emerged as a barrier to continued studies. The cost of a PhD, particularly the loss of earnings, deterred these burgeoning academics from continuing.

## Policy implications and future research directions

This research has clear policy implications for equality agendas in schooling, higher education and industry. The strained relationships between African-Caribbean parents and schools suggest that schools need to engage black parents about their children's educational rather than behavioural issues and that black parents should more actively support and encourage their children in their schoolwork (Education Commission, 2004). McKenley (2005) observes the need for research into parental involvement that is undertaken from the parents' viewpoint and located within black communities. This could complement the types of outreach initiatives outlined by Rhamie (2007), such as workshops and courses that encourage black parents to become involved in their children's schooling and equip them to have a positive impact.

Drawing these points together, I suggest that we need initiatives designed to empower black parents not only to encourage and help their children with schoolwork but also to challenge injustice within schools in a constructive way. Schools should be encouraged to be welcoming and receptive to black parents so they can respond to the parents' perceptions of the issues. An approach that incorporates shared responsibility would enable parents and schools to work towards the same goal of improving the educational experiences of black children and therefore their outcomes.

Negative racial stereotyping is the modern-day manifestation of scientific racism and the insidious nature of such thinking makes it difficult but vital to challenge in educational settings. One of the most effective strategies for tackling racist stereotyping and raising achievement for minoritized pupils is increasing the presence of minoritized and anti-racist teachers in schools (Arbouin, 1989; Education Commission, 2004). We need to be training practitioners and rethinking the monocultural school curriculum, so that our educational institutions reflect a worldview and the diversity of the school and UK population. Rejecting school can be a means of students maintaining self-esteem in an environment that denigrates their own culture (Channer, 1995; Mac an Ghaill, 1988). Consequently, in order to reinforce positive self-esteem, schools need to take responsibility for teaching black children about the contributions that black and minoritized people and cultures have made to society. It is equally important that children from all ethnicities learn to value and respect black and minoritized cultures. The same applies to further and higher educational institutions.

This research highlighted an apparent predisposition for black students to turn to black academic staff for support. It is, therefore, incumbent upon higher educational institutions to allocate resources for diversity training that will make staff more accessible to black students, and to recognize the ways black staff support black students. Increasing the number of black lecturers in higher education would both support black students and facilitate understanding between black students and white staff. Their presence alone would begin to break down certain deeply embedded barriers.

Despite my participants' concerns about isolation in higher education, it appears that their actual experience of higher education was less isolating than they had expected. The prospect of not fitting in had greatest impact as a psychological barrier before they started university. Policy designed to eliminate these fears will be most effective if the universities' promotional literature describes the support networks that would most appeal to minoritized students, such as African-Caribbean Societies.

The growing number of black people who embark upon self-employment to circumvent organizational politics will contribute to greater prosperity within black communities in the UK (BBC Radio 4, 2006). Black Britons are more likely to consider self-employment (Nelson, 2004), but poor access to funding is a major hindrance (DTI, 2003; Maurey, 2005). Participants in my research identified financial difficulties relating to set-up costs and cash flow as key stumbling blocks to their entrepreneurial ideas. To tackle the multiplier effect of race, gender and class bias faced by many black would-be entrepreneurs, policies should be implemented to (a) target funding for fairer distribution across ethnicities, (b) target funding for female entrepreneurs, who tend to have less access to savings than men and (c) earmark regeneration funding for applicants residing in regeneration areas.

Appropriate business mentors are an asset to new businesses (Nelson, 2004) but every member of my cohort of young entrepreneurs said they had no business mentor for their fledgling enterprises and found this to be problematic. Initiatives designed to encourage highly qualified and skilled minoritized people to be mentors could facilitate business start-ups among black graduates and help them develop their business management skills.

In terms of future research directions, I would argue that the black women in my research represent an untapped resource in academic life. The women participants evidenced a combination of academic ability, strong inclination towards learning in higher education, and a love of their academic subject. Universities, governments and charities who profess their commitment to tackling inequity could harness such talent by directing funding towards research that gives voice to black women's experiences and perspectives, embracing race, class and gender issues. This could attract black women into the academic community and increase social inclusion by tackling: (a) the under-representation of black and female academic staff; and (b) the need for more diverse perspectives and curricula in higher education institutions.

The participants in this research represent part of a growing pool of professionally qualified and skilled black workers in Britain, who are achieving in the face of societal structures that limit their options. Inequalities in the workplace waste their talents and abilities. However, it has stimulated their inclination towards entrepreneurial and community endeavours and their potential should be harnessed and put to good use in regenerating communities. Increasing business ownership among black graduates would also provide more role models to encourage future generations of black workers into enterprise and education. So, clearly, investment in black graduates such as these would help to build vibrant communities and a stronger UK economy.

To achieve this goal, research is needed to investigate ways to channel the skills and motivation of black graduates like my participants into building stronger, healthier communities and maximizing social inclusion in both education and careers. Further research into the relationship between educational success and community activism within black communities would develop the understanding of how the conscientization of black graduates can stimulate the activism that challenges inequalities and builds communities.

## Conclusions

In this book I have drawn upon the existing literature on race, class and gender in education and employment to outline the structural trajectory of ten black graduates across these domains. The narratives of the research participants, who generously gave their time, added depth and insight. The theoretical framework drew upon reproduction theory, critical race theory, black feminist theory and the theory of intersectionality to address the research questions. The responses to the three research questions can be summarized as follows:

### How do black graduates experience the structures of race, class and gender in employment and educational settings?

Despite starting well in compulsory schooling, socio-economic factors positioned participants in poorly resourced inner city schools. Negative racial stereotyping by their teachers manifested as low expectations for girls and conflict for boys, and ultimately hindered their ability and inclination to achieve their full potential. The girls typically remained oriented to school and qualifications, and left school with two to three GCSE equivalents. Boys typically immersed themselves in their peer group and sporting endeavours, and left school with no good GCSE equivalents.

Progression through post-compulsory education was slow in comparison to the typical middle-class trajectory and most of my participants pursued non-traditional paths to higher education. The financial burden of studying was the main deterrent to continuing education. A number of participants in higher education felt that lecturers gave them little support, and microaggressions tainted their experience. The power dynamics of teacher–student relationships ensured that they suffered in silence and they used emotional withdrawal to survive. The lack of diversity in staffing and the Eurocentric curriculum added to their sense of 'un-belonging' and many suffered from fear of failure.

In employment, the participants were concentrated in the public sector, where equality of opportunity informs recruitment. Teaching emerged as the default career, reflecting the class dynamic, as it offered accessible funding and direct entry into professional employment. Teaching also offered the mothers a relatively easy fit with childcare responsibilities. However, entry did not guarantee progression and the participants' careers seemed to plateau at an early stage in their professions, suggesting an ethnic penalty and/or sticky floor syndrome. Official and unofficial disputes punctuated the careers of those whose organizational life was rooted in their outsider status.

### What resources do black graduates draw upon to navigate these domains and enable their successes?

Only two participants achieved school success and the disparity between their experiences made conclusive analysis of the contributory factors impossible. However, features that generally enhanced participants' school experiences included black teachers who were particularly supportive and fair with black pupils, and family discourses that cite education as a key to success.

The participants' routes to higher education either involved a series of stepping stones to compensate for their lack of school leaving qualifications, or they experienced a transition of some sort. They identified people who acted as catalysts and these included peers, managers or church leaders, who were mostly black or immersed in black communities. The same was true in higher education, where minoritized teaching staff provided additional support and encouragement. Primary motivations to study in higher education revolved around social mobility and family expectations. The pleasure of studying was particularly important among the women, whose love of learning tended to sustain their studies to postgraduate level. Participants used their unique African-Caribbean social capital, by tapping into black social networks such as family, church and African-Caribbean Societies, in order to overcome their sense of isolation in higher education.

In the face of obstacles to career progression, many interviewees saw entrepreneurialism as an alternative to traditional employment, offering the potential to avoid organizational politics and balance childcare commitments with earning potential. Self-employment shifted the emphasis in the workplace from people dynamics to the participants' ability to perform the job well.

### *In what ways do black graduates consider it important to use their skills and experiences to challenge the inequalities of race, class and gender in British society?*

Many of my participants sought to challenge the inequalities of race, class and gender by serving the community, seeing it as a way to 'give back' to the black community. This suggests a process of conscientization. Service to the community linked with entrepreneurial ideas aimed at catering to black community needs. Career choices reflected a preference for working in schools that served black and working-class children, although this could mean forfeiting opportunities to work in prestigious institutions. The participants also served their community through voluntary endeavours such as Saturday schools and mentoring. Several women expressed interest in conducting PhD research into issues pertinent to black communities and women, but the opportunity cost of a PhD was prohibitive.

Most participants saw the need for proportional representation of women in academic posts at various levels within higher education and felt that the core curriculum should include a feminist perspective.

This final chapter has highlighted certain policy implications that suggest the need to:

- implement initiatives to improve communications between black parents and schools
- appoint more minoritized and anti-racist staff in teaching and key roles in schools, post-compulsory education and higher education in order to improve diversity among educators
- increase and improve diversity training for all educators so that negative racial stereotyping is tackled at all levels of education
- introduce a diverse curriculum at each stage of the education process to reflect a more holistic worldview and the diversity of the UK population
- invest in improved support for black staff and black students in higher education institutions, to deal with the additional pressures and barriers they encounter on account of their ethnicity
- publish promotional literature for each institution that informs potential students about the black social networks they can tap into for support
- increase funding for tackling race, class and gender bias in business start-ups
- improve access to mentoring provision for minoritized entrepreneurs by targeting their needs.

The book has identified the need for further research to:

- develop initiatives that could encourage community and entrepreneurial endeavours among black graduates so that they can make full use of their skills and training and help to build stronger communities for future generations
- find ways to harness the potential contribution of the untapped resource of black women as researchers in higher education
- explore the process of conscientization among black graduates so they can continue to challenge inequalities in British society.

# Appendix: Participant biographies[1]

## Alison

| | |
|---|---|
| Parents' island of origin: | St Kitts |
| Father's occupation[2]: | Minister of religion |
| Mother's occupation: | Seamstress |
| Graduate parent(s): | Father |
| Participant's age[3]: | 40 |
| Male/female: | Female |
| School type/location: | State; city |
| School leaving qualifications[4]: | 2 or 3 GCSE equivalents[5] |
| Graduate/professional qualifications: | BA (Hons) Combined Arts<br>Cert of English Language Teaching to Adults<br>Dip for English Language Teaching to Adults<br>MA in English Language Teaching |
| Occupation: | HE lecturer |
| Marital status: | Unmarried[6] |
| No. of children: | None |
| Location: | Midlands |

## Notes

[1] Details recorded here reflect participants' circumstances and information provided at the time of the primary data collection. Some details may have changed since then.

[2] Parents' main occupation during participant's childhood education.

[3] At end of primary data collection.

[4] At end of compulsory schooling.

[5] Grades A* to C.

[6] I have used the term 'unmarried', rather than 'single', as some participants were co-habiting in long-term relationships although they were not married.

# Elaine

| | |
|---|---|
| Parents' island of origin: | Jamaica |
| Father's occupation: | Taxi driver |
| Mother's occupation: | Teacher |
| Graduate parent(s): | Mother |
| Participant's age: | 43 |
| Male/female: | Female |
| School type/location: | State; village |
| School leaving qualifications: | 7 GCSE equivalents |
| Graduate/professional qualifications: | BA (Hons) Hispanic Studies |
| Occupation: | Self-employed consultant |
| Marital status: | Married |
| No. of children: | 5 |
| Location: | Midlands |

# Eve

| | |
|---|---|
| Parents' island of origin: | St Kitts |
| Father's occupation: | Unknown |
| Mother's occupation: | At home mother |
| Graduate parent(s): | None |
| Participant's age: | 40 |
| Male/female: | Female |
| School type/location: | State; city |
| School leaving qualifications: | 2 or 3 GCSE equivalents |
| Graduate/professional qualifications: | BA (Hons) Religious Studies MA in Religion and Public Life PGCE |
| Occupation: | Self-employed hairdresser/school teacher (secondary) |
| Marital status: | Unmarried |
| No. of children: | None |
| Location: | Midlands |

# Michelle

| | |
|---|---|
| Parents' island of origin: | Jamaica |
| Father's occupation: | Unknown |
| Mother's occupation: | Unknown |
| Graduate parent(s): | None |
| Participant's age: | 38 |
| Male/female: | Female |
| School type/location: | State; city |
| School leaving qualifications: | 3 GCSE equivalents |
| Graduate/professional qualifications: | BSc (Hons) Export Engineering PGCE MSc in IT for Manufacture |
| Occupation: | School teacher (secondary) |
| Marital status: | Unmarried |
| No. of children: | 2 |
| Location: | London |

# Nora

| | |
|---|---|
| Parents' island of origin: | St Kitts |
| Father's occupation: | Unknown |
| Mother's occupation: | At home mother |
| Graduate parent(s): | None |
| Participant's age: | 39 |
| Male/female: | Female |
| School type/location: | State; city |
| School leaving qualifications: | 2 or 3 GCSE equivalents |
| Graduate/ professional qualifications: | BA (Hons) Psychology PGCE MA in Education Management |
| Occupation: | Headteacher (primary) |
| Marital status: | Unmarried |
| No. of children: | 2 |
| Location: | London |

# Dean

| | |
|---|---|
| Parents' island of origin: | Jamaica |
| Father's occupation: | Unknown |
| Mother's occupation: | Unknown |
| Graduate parent(s): | None |
| Participant's age: | 37 |
| Male/female: | Male |
| School type/location: | State; city |
| School leaving qualifications: | No GCSE equivalents |
| Graduate/professional qualifications: | BA (Hons) Combined Community and Youth Studies |
| Occupation: | Youth worker |
| Marital status: | Unmarried |
| No. of children: | None |
| Location: | London/Midlands |

# Leroy

| | |
|---|---|
| Parents' island of origin: | Jamaica |
| Father's occupation: | Unknown |
| Mother's occupation: | Dinner lady |
| Graduate parent(s): | None |
| Participant's age: | 38 |
| Male/female: | Male |
| School type/location: | State; city |
| School leaving qualifications: | 6 GCSE equivalents |
| Graduate/professional qualifications: | BA (Hons) Product and Furniture Design PGCE |
| Occupation: | FE lecturer |
| Marital status: | Unmarried |
| No. of children: | 2 |
| Location: | London |

# Neil

| | |
|---|---|
| Parents' island of origin: | Jamaica |
| Father's occupation: | Bus driver |
| Mother's occupation: | Dressmaker at home |
| Graduate parent(s): | None |
| Participant's age: | 42 |
| Male/female: | Male |
| School type/location: | State; city |
| School leaving qualifications: | No GCSE equivalents |
| Graduate/professional qualifications: | HND in Computer Technology<br>Certificate of Education in FE<br>PG Diploma in Management Studies<br>MA in Human Resources<br>PG Diploma in Project Management |
| Occupation: | FE lecturer/IT trainer |
| Marital status: | Unmarried |
| No. of children: | None |
| Location: | London |

# Sean

| | |
|---|---|
| Parents' island of origin: | Jamaica |
| Father's occupation: | Unskilled worker |
| Mother's occupation: | Unskilled worker |
| Graduate parent(s): | None |
| Participant's age: | 40 |
| Male/female: | Male |
| School type/location: | State; city |
| School leaving qualifications: | No GCSE equivalents |
| Graduate/professional qualifications: | BA (Hons) Sociology |
| Occupation: | Housing advice manager |
| Marital status: | Unmarried |
| No. of children: | 3 |
| Location: | Midlands |

# Zac

| | |
|---|---|
| **Parents' island of origin:** | Jamaica |
| **Father's occupation:** | Factory worker |
| **Mother's occupation:** | Nurse |
| **Graduate parent(s):** | None |
| **Participant's age:** | 38 |
| **Male/female:** | Male |
| **School type/location:** | State; city |
| **School leaving qualifications:** | No GCSE equivalents |
| **Graduate/professional qualifications:** | BA (Hons) Three Dimensional Design |
| **Occupation:** | Self-employed – multimedia promotions |
| **Marital status:** | Married |
| **No. of children:** | 1 |
| **Location:** | Midlands |

# References

Abbott, D. (2002) 'Teachers are failing black boys'. *The Guardian*, 6 January. Online. www.theguardian.com/politics/2002/jan/06/publicservices.race (accessed 10 January 2017).

Acland, T. and Azmi, W. (1998) 'Expectation and reality: Ethnic minorities in higher education'. In Modood, T. and Acland, T. (eds) *Race and Higher Education: Experiences, challenges and policy implications*. London: Policy Studies Institute, 74–85.

Alfred, M.V. (1997) 'A reconceptualisation of marginality: Perspectives of African-American female faculty in the white academy'. In *Crossing Borders, Breaking Boundaries: Research in the education of adults*. Proceedings of the 27th Annual SCUTREA Conference, London, 1–3 July 1997. Online. www.leeds.ac.uk/educol/documents/000000195.htm (accessed 18 August 2017).

Allen, A. (1998) 'What are ethnic minorities looking for?'. In Modood, T. and Acland, T. (eds) *Race and Higher Education: Experiences, challenges and policy implications*. London: Policy Studies Institute, 51–73.

Allen, P.M. (1998) 'Towards a black construct of accessibility'. In Modood, T. and Acland, T. (eds) *Race and Higher Education: Experiences, challenges and policy implications*. London: Policy Studies Institute, 86–95.

Arbouin, L. (1989) 'Some factors influencing Afro-Caribbean pupils' academic success in the secondary school: A case study'. Unpublished MA thesis, University of York.

Archer, L. and Francis, B. (2007) *Understanding Minority Ethnic Achievement: Race, gender, class and "success"*. London: Routledge.

Asher, N. (2001) 'Beyond "cool" and "hip": Engaging the question of research and writing as academic self-woman of color other'. *International Journal of Qualitative Studies in Education*, 14 (1), 1–12.

Atewologun, 'D. and Singh, V. (2010) 'Challenging ethnic and gender identities: An exploration of UK black professionals' identity construction'. *Equality, Diversity and Inclusion: An International Journal*, 29 (4), 332–47.

Ball, S.J., Reay, D. and David, M. (2002) '"Ethnic choosing": Minority ethnic students, social class and higher education choice'. *Race Ethnicity and Education*, 5 (4), 333–57.

Barclays SME Research Team (2005) *Black and Minority Ethnic Business Owners: A market research perspective*. London: Barclays Bank.

BBC Radio 4 (2006) *The Black Middle Classes*. 15 and 22 January. London: BBC.

BCU (Birmingham City University) (2017) 'Black Studies – BA (Hons)'. Online. www.bcu.ac.uk/courses/black-studies-ba-hons-2017-18 (accessed 25 April 2017).

Bell, E.L. (1990) 'The bicultural life experience of career-oriented black women'. *Journal of Organizational Behavior*, 11 (6), 459–77.

Bell, J. (1993) *Doing Your Research Project: A guide for first-time researchers in education and social sciences*. 2nd ed. Buckinghamshire: Open University Press.

Bird, J. (1996) *Black Students and Higher Education: Rhetorics and realities.* Buckingham: Society for Research into Higher Education/Open University Press.

Blanchflower, D.G. and Shadforth, C. (2007) 'Entrepreneurship in the UK'. *Foundations and Trends in Entrepreneurship*, 3 (4), 257–364. Online. www. nowpublishers.com/article/Details/ENT-017 (accessed 12 April 2017).

BLINK (Black Information Link) (2005) *A Black Manifesto for Equality in Our Lifetime.* Online. www.naar.org.uk/resources/PDFs/BlackManifesto2005.pdf (accessed 31 December 2007).

Boliver, V. (2013) 'How fair is access to more prestigious UK universities?'. *British Journal of Sociology*, 64 (2), 344–64.

— (2015) 'Are there distinctive clusters of higher and lower status universities in the UK?'. *Oxford Review of Education*, 41 (5), 608–27.

Bourdieu, P. and Passeron, J.-C. (1994) *Reproduction in Education, Society and Culture.* Trans. Nice, R. 2nd ed. London: SAGE Publications.

Bourdieu, P. and Wacquant, L.J.D. (1992) *An Invitation to Reflexive Sociology.* Cambridge: Polity Press.

Brah, A. and Phoenix, A. (2004) 'Ain't I a woman? Revisiting intersectionality'. *Journal of International Women's Studies*, 5 (3), 75–86.

Bravette, G. (1996) 'Reflections on a black woman's management learning'. *Women in Management Review*, 11 (3), 3–11.

Bryan, B., Dadzie, S. and Scafe, S. (1985) *The Heart of the Race: Black women's lives in Britain.* London: Virago Press.

Burgess, S. and Greaves, E. (2009) *Test Scores, Subjective Assessment and Stereotyping of Ethnic Minorities* (Working Paper 09/221). Bristol: Centre for Market and Public Organisation.

Butler, J. (1990) *Gender Trouble: Feminism and the subversion of identity.* New York: Routledge.

— (1993) *Bodies that Matter: On the discursive limits of 'sex'.* London and New York: Routledge.

Casey, K. (1993) *I Answer with My Life: Life histories of women teachers working for social change.* New York: Routledge.

Channel 4 Television (2006) *30 Minutes.* 'Does feminism offer today's women an unrealistic dream of independence?' 3 February. London: Channel 4.

Channer, Y. (1995) *I am a Promise: The school achievement of British African Caribbeans.* Stoke-on-Trent: Trentham Books.

Channer, Y. and Franklin, A. (1995) '"Race", curriculum and HE: Black lecturers' reflections'. *Journal of Further and Higher Education*, 19 (3), 32–46.

CI Research (2006) *Ethnic Minority Businesses in West Yorkshire: Research to identify current characteristics of ethnic minority businesses and to understand their needs and aspirations.* UK: West Yorkshire Economic Partnership.

Coard, B. (1971) *How the West Indian Child is Made Educationally Sub-Normal in the British School System.* London: New Beacon Books.

Coleman, N.A.T. (2015) 'Diversity is a dirty word.' Paper presented at the Developing Diversity Competence – 2nd Annual Equality Challenge Unit (ECU) and Higher Education Academy (HEA) Scotland Conference, Our Dynamic Earth, Edinburgh, April 2015.

Collins, P.H. (1986) 'Learning from the outsider within: The sociological significance of black feminist thought'. *Social Problems*, 33 (6), S14–32.

— (2000) *Black Feminist Thought: Knowledge, consciousness, and the politics of empowerment.* 2nd ed. New York: Routledge.

Crenshaw, K. (1991) 'Mapping the margins: Intersectionality, identity politics, and violence against women of color'. *Stanford Law Review*, 43 (6), 1241–99.

Critical 2 Limited (2005) *Health, Wealth and Happiness: Is Britain really an "enterprise culture"?* UK: MORE TH>N Business.

Dabydeen, D., Gilmore, J. and Jones, C. (eds) (2007) *The Oxford Companion to Black British History.* Oxford: Oxford University Press.

Dawe, A., Fielden, S. and Woolnough, H. (2006) *A Pilot Study to Investigate the Accessibility of Business Finance for Small and Medium Sized Enterprises in the North West.* Manchester: University of Manchester Institute of Science and Technology.

Dearing, R. (1997) *Higher Education in the Learning Society: Report of the National Committee of Inquiry into Higher Education.* London: HMSO.

Desforges, C. and Abouchaar, A. (2003) *The Impact of Parental Involvement, Parental Support and Family Education on Pupil Achievement and Adjustment: A literature review* (Research Report 433). Nottingham: Department for Education and Skills.

DfE (Department for Education) (2015) *Statistical First Release: GCSE and equivalent attainment by pupil characteristics, 2013 to 2014 (Revised).* London: Department for Education. Online. www.gov.uk/government/uploads/ system/uploads/attachment_data/file/399005/SFR06_2015_Text.pdf (accessed 18 August 2017).

DfES (Department for Education and Skills) (2003) *Aiming High: Raising the achievement of minority ethnic pupils.* Nottingham: Department for Education and Skills.

DTI (Department of Trade and Industry) (2003) *A Strategic Framework for Women's Enterprise.* London: Department of Trade and Industry.

Du Bois, W.E.B. (2000 [1903]) *The Souls of Black Folk.* Bensenville: Lushena Classics.

ECU (Equality Challenge Unit) (2014) *Equality in Higher Education: Statistical report 2014.* London: Equality Challenge Unit. Online. www.ecu.ac.uk/ publications/equality-higher-education-statistical-report-2014/ (accessed 18 August 2017).

Education Commission (2004) *The Educational Experiences and Achievements of Black Boys in London Schools, 2000–2003.* London: London Development Agency.

EHRC (Equality and Human Rights Commission) (2011) *How Fair is Britain? Equality, human rights and good relations in 2010: The first triennial review.* London: Equality and Human Rights Commission. Online. www. equalityhumanrights.com/sites/default/files/how_fair_is_britain_-_complete_ report.pdf (accessed 1 August 2016).

— (2015) *Is Britain Fairer? The state of equality and human rights 2015.* London: Equality and Human Rights Commission. Online. www.equalityhumanrights. com/en/britain-fairer (accessed 8 April 2017).

# References

Elias, P., McKnight, A., Purcell, K. and Wilson, R. (1997) *A Study of the Labour Market for Social Science Postgraduates*. Coventry: Institute for Employment Research, University of Warwick.

Elmes, J. (2015) 'Q&A with Tracey Reynolds'. *Times Higher Education*, 14 May. Online. www.timeshighereducation.com/news/people/qa-with-tracey-reynolds/2020139.article (accessed 18 August 2017).

Evans, G. (2006) *Educational Failure and Working Class White Children in Britain*. Basingstoke: Palgrave Macmillan.

Fanon, F. (1986) *Black Skin, White Masks*. London: Pluto Press.

Freire, P. (1972) *Cultural Action for Freedom*. New York: Penguin Books.

— (1996) *Pedagogy of the Oppressed*. Trans. Ramos, M.B. London: Penguin Books.

Gazeley, L. and Dunne, M. (2005) *Addressing Working Class Underachievement*. Brighton: University of Sussex.

Gilkes, C.T. (1982) 'Successful rebellious professionals: The black woman's professional identity and community commitment'. *Psychology of Women Quarterly*, 6 (3), 289–311.

Gillborn, D. (1990) *'Race', Ethnicity and Education: Teaching and learning in multi-ethnic schools*. London: Unwin Hyman.

— (1998) 'Race and ethnicity in compulsory schooling'. In Modood, T. and Acland, T. (eds) *Race and Higher Education: Experiences, challenges and policy implications*. London: Policy Studies Institute, 11–23.

— (2005) 'Education policy as an act of white supremacy: Whiteness, critical race theory and education reform'. *Journal of Education Policy*, 20 (4), 485–505.

Glaser, B.G. and Strauss, A.L. (1967) *The Discovery of Grounded Theory: Strategies for qualitative research*. Chicago: Aldine de Gruyter.

Glenn, E.N. (2002) *Unequal Freedom: How race and gender shaped American citizenship and labor*. Cambridge, MA: Harvard University Press.

Gordon, G. (2007) *Towards Bicultural Competence: Beyond black and white*. Stoke-on-Trent: Trentham Books.

Graham, M. (2001) 'The "miseducation" of black children in the British educational system: Towards an African-centred orientation to knowledge'. In Majors, R. (ed.) *Educating Our Black Children: New directions and radical approaches*. London: RoutledgeFalmer, 61–78.

Graham, M. and Robinson, G. (2004) '"The silent catastrophe": Institutional racism in the British educational system and the underachievement of black boys'. *Journal of Black Studies*, 34 (5), 653–71.

HESA (Higher Education Statistics Agency) (1998) 'Students in higher education 1996/97'. Online. www.hesa.ac.uk/data-and-analysis/publications/students-1996-97 (accessed 18 August 2017).

— (2008) 'View statistics online'. Online. www.hesa.ac.uk (accessed 10 March 2009).

— (2011) 'Staff in higher education 2009/10'. Online. www.hesa.ac.uk/data-and-analysis/publications/staff-2009-10 (accessed 18 August 2017).

hooks, b. (1989) *Talking Back: Thinking feminist, thinking black*. London: Sheba Feminist Press.

— (1993) *Sisters of the Yam: Black women and self-recovery*. Boston: South End Press.

— (1994) *Teaching to Transgress: Education as the practice of freedom.* New York: Routledge.

— (1996) *Killing Rage: Ending racism.* London: Penguin Books.

hooks, b. and West, C. (1991) *Breaking Bread: Insurgent black intellectual life.* Boston: South End Press.

Hughes, C. (2002) *Women's Contemporary Lives: Within and beyond the mirror.* London: Routledge.

Hughes, C., Perrier, M. and Kramer, A.-M. (2007). 'Plaisir et jouissance: Intellectual life, the student and pleasure'. Paper presented at the iPED 2007 Conference, Coventry University, September 2007.

Hutchinson, J., Rolfe, H., Moore, N., Bysshe, S. and Bentley, K. (2011) *All Things Being Equal? Equality and diversity in careers education, information, advice and guidance* (Research Report 71). London: Equality and Human Rights Commission. Online. www.equalityhumanrights.com/sites/default/files/research-report-71-all_things-being-equal-equality-and-diversity-in-careers-education-information-and-advice.pdf (accessed 18 August 2017).

Jackson, C. (2002) '"Laddishness" as a self-worth protection strategy'. *Gender and Education*, 14 (1), 37–51.

Jiwani, A. and Regan, T. (1998) 'Race, culture and the curriculum'. In Modood, T. and Acland, T. (eds) *Race and Higher Education: Experiences, challenges and policy implications.* London: Policy Studies Institute, 96–111.

Joseph, G.I. and Lewis, J. (1986) *Common Differences: Conflicts in black and white feminist perspectives.* Boston: South End Press.

Karenga, M. (1993) *Introduction to Black Studies.* 2nd ed. Los Angeles, CA: The University of Sankore Press.

Kennedy, H. (1997) *Learning Works: Widening participation in further education.* Coventry: Further Education Funding Council.

Knowles, M.S., Holton, E.F. and Swanson, R.A. (1998) *The Adult Learner: The definitive classic in adult education and human resource development.* 5th ed. Houston: Gulf Publishing Company.

Ladson-Billings, G. (2005) 'The evolving role of critical race theory in educational scholarship'. *Race Ethnicity and Education*, 8 (1), 115–19.

LDA (London Development Agency) (2005) *Redefining London's BME-Owned Businesses.* London: London Development Agency.

Leicester, M. and Merrill, B. (1999) *Antiracist Adult Education: Lifelong learning in a pluralist society.* Nottingham: Continuing Education Press.

Mac an Ghaill, M. (1988) *Young, Gifted and Black: Student–teacher relations in the schooling of black youth.* Milton Keynes: Open University Press.

Mandhai, S. (2017) 'UK students push for more non-white thinkers on courses'. *Al Jazeera*, 13 January. Online. www.aljazeera.com/news/2017/01/uk-students-push-white-thinkers-courses-170113145608896.html (accessed 31 January 2017).

Maurey, K. (2005) 'The growth of black and ethnic minority women in business'. *Prowess Profile: Journal for Women's Enterprise*, 5, 7–9.

Mayor, V. (2002) *Staying Power: The career journeys of leading African, African-Caribbean and Asian nurses in England.* PhD thesis, University of Warwick.

Mbandaka, Bro. Ldr. (2004) *Education: An Afrikan-centred approach to excellence.* UK: Soul Force Promotions.

# References

McGivney, V. (2004) *Men Earn, Women Learn: Bridging the gender divide in education and training*. Leicester: National Institute of Adult Continuing Education.

McKay, A., Campbell, J., Thomson, E. and Ross, S. (2013) 'Economic recession and recovery in the UK: What's gender got to do with it?'. *Feminist Economics*, 19 (3), 108–23.

McKenley, J. (2005) *Seven Black Men: An ecological study of education and parenting*. Bristol: Aduma Books.

McKernan, J. (1991) *Curriculum Action Research*. London: Kogan Page.

Mirza, H.S. (1992) *Young, Female and Black*. London: Routledge.

— (1997) *Black British Feminism: A reader*. London: Routledge.

— (2005) *'Dynamite Misses' – Young Black Women and Education*. Listening to Black and Ethnic Minority Women's Voices Seminar Report, June 2005. UK: Fawcett Women.

Modood, T. and Acland, T. (eds) (1998) *Race and Higher Education: Experiences, challenges and policy implications*. London: Policy Studies Institute.

Modood, T., Berthoud, R., Lakey, J., Nazroo, J., Smith, P., Virdee, S. and Beishon, S. (1997) *Ethnic Minorities in Britain: Diversity and disadvantage*. London: Policy Studies Institute.

Mogadime, D. (2003) 'Contradictions in feminist pedagogy: Black women students' perspectives'. *Resources for Feminist Research*, 30 (1–2), 7–32.

Moore, T. (1992) *Care of the Soul: How to add depth and meaning to your everyday life*. London: Piatkus.

Morris, E.W. (2007) '"Ladies" or "loudies"? Perceptions and experiences of black girls in classrooms'. *Youth and Society*, 38 (4), 490–515.

Mukherjee, A.P. (2001) 'In but not at home: Women of colour in the academy'. *Resources for Feminist Research*, 29 (1–2), 125–35.

Nelson, M. (2004) *Patience and Partnership: Successfully supporting women entrepreneurs in the United Kingdom*. UK: Women's Business Development Agency.

Nightingale, D.J. and Cromby, J. (eds) (1999) *Social Constructionist Psychology: A critical analysis of theory and practice*. Buckingham: Open University Press.

Odih, P. (2002) 'Mentors and role models: Masculinity and the educational "underachievement" of young Afro-Caribbean males'. *Race Ethnicity and Education*, 5 (1), 91–105.

Omar, A., Davidson, M.J., Fielden, S., Hunt, C. and Dawe, A.J. (2004) *A Pilot Study To Investigate the Problems, Experiences and Barriers Faced by a Cross Section of Black and Ethnic Minority Female Entrepreneurs (SMEs) in the North West*. Manchester: University of Manchester Institute of Science and Technology.

Osborne, J.W. (2001) 'Academic disidentification: Unravelling underachievement among black boys'. In Majors, R. (ed.) *Educating Our Black Children: New directions and radical approaches*. London: RoutledgeFalmer, 45–58.

Pearce, S. (2005) *You Wouldn't Understand: White teachers in multi-ethnic classrooms*. Stoke-on-Trent: Trentham Books.

Pomeroy, E. (1999) 'The teacher–student relationship in secondary school: Insights from excluded students'. *British Journal of Sociology of Education*, 20 (4), 465–82.

Powell, F. (1999) 'Adult education, cultural empowerment and social equality: The Cork Northside Education Initiative'. *Widening Participation and Lifelong Learning*, 1 (1), 20–6.

Prowess (2005) 'Learning from Sweden'. *Prowess Profile: Journal for Women's Enterprise*, 5, 16.

Purcell, K. (ed.) (2000) *Changing Boundaries in Employment*. Bristol: Bristol Academic Press.

Reay, D. (2001) 'Finding or losing yourself? Working-class relationships to education'. *Journal of Education Policy*, 16 (4), 333–46.

— (2002) 'Shaun's story: Troubling discourses of white working-class masculinities'. *Gender and Education*, 14 (3), 221–34.

— (2003) 'A risky business? Mature working-class women students and access to higher education'. *Gender and Education*, 15 (3), 301–17.

Reynolds, T. (1997) '(Mis)representing the black (super)woman'. In Mirza, H.S. (ed.) *Black British Feminism: A reader*. London: Routledge, 97–112.

— (2006) 'Supporting student learning of black Caribbean male students in the Faculty of Art Humanities and Science'. Unpublished: South Bank University.

Rhamie, J. (2007) *Eagles Who Soar: How black learners find the path to success*. Stoke-on-Trent: Trentham Books.

Rhamie, J. and Hallam, S. (2002) 'An investigation into African-Caribbean academic success in the UK'. *Race Ethnicity and Education*, 5 (2), 151–70.

Richardson, B. (ed.) (2005) *Tell It Like It Is: How our schools fail black children*. London: Bookmarks/Trentham Books.

Ritchie, J. and Lewis, J. (eds) (2003) *Qualitative Research Practice: A guide for social science students and researchers*. London: Sage Publications Limited.

Robinson, G. (2007) 'The coping strategies of black people who are managers in public sector organisations'. Paper presented at the African Centred Research Colloquium, London South Bank University, July 2007.

Rodgers, A. (2006) 'Mentoring and writing workshops first year students on the SPS Scheme'. Paper presented at the FAHS Equality and Diversity Committee Research Seminar, London South Bank University, 30 November 2006.

Rollock, N., Gillborn, D., Vincent, C. and Ball, S.J. (2015) *The Colour of Class: The educational strategies of the black middle classes*. London: Routledge.

Savage, M. (2015) *Social Class in the 21st Century*. London: Pelican Books.

Sewell, T. (1997) *Black Masculinities and Schooling: How black boys survive modern schooling*. Stoke-on-Trent: Trentham Books.

Singh, Gurharpal (1998) 'Race equality staffing policies in higher education'. In Modood, T. and Acland, T. (eds) *Race and Higher Education: Experiences, challenges and policy implications*. London: Policy Studies Institute, 144–57.

Singh, Gurnham (2004) 'Anti-racist social work, context and development: Refracted through the experience of black practice teachers'. Unpublished PhD thesis, University of Warwick, Coventry.

Skelton, C. (2001) *Schooling the Boys: Masculinities and primary education*. Buckingham: Open University Press.

Solórzano, D.G. (1998) 'Critical race theory, race and gender microaggressions, and the experience of Chicana and Chicano scholars'. *International Journal of Qualitative Studies in Education*, 11 (1), 121–36.

Taylor, P. (1992) 'Ethnic group data and applications to higher education'. *Higher Education Quarterly*, 46 (4), 359–74.

TUC (Trades Union Congress) (2015a) *Living on the Margins: Black workers and casualisation*. London: Trades Union Congress. Online. www.tuc.org.uk/sites/default/files/LivingontheMargins.pdf (accessed 12 April 2017).

— (2015b) *The Impact on Women of Recession and Austerity*. London: Trades Union Congress. Online. www.tuc.org.uk/sites/default/files/WomenRecession.pdf (accessed 18 August 2017).

— (2016) 'Black workers with degrees earn a quarter less than white counterparts, finds TUC'. Press release, 1 February. Online. www.tuc.org.uk/equality-issues/black-workers/labour-market/black-workers-degrees-earn-quarter-less-white (accessed 24 January 2017).

Van Dyke, R. (1998) 'Monitoring the progress and achievement of ethnic minority students: A new methodology'. In Modood, T. and Acland, T. (eds) *Race and Higher Education: Experiences, challenges and policy implications*. London: Policy Studies Institute, 115–33.

Vincent, C., Rollock, N., Ball, S. and Gillborn, D. (2011) *The Educational Strategies of the Black Middle Classes: Project summary*. London: Institute of Education. Online. www.birmingham.ac.uk/Documents/college-social-sciences/education/research-centres/black-middle-classes-summary.pdf (accessed 18 August 2017).

Wingfield, A.H. (2011) *Changing Times for Black Professionals*. New York: Routledge.

Wright, C., Thompson, S. and Channer, Y. (2007) 'Out of place: Black women academics in British universities'. *Women's History Review*, 16 (2), 145–62.

Wright, C., Weekes, D., McGlaughlin, A. and Webb, D. (1998) 'Masculinised discourses within education and the construction of black male identities amongst African Caribbean youth'. *British Journal of Sociology of Education*, 19 (1), 75–87.

Yosso, T.J. (2005) 'Whose culture has capital? A critical race theory discussion of community cultural wealth'. *Race Ethnicity and Education*, 8 (1), 69–91.

Young, M.F.D. (1971) 'An approach to the study of curricula as socially organized knowledge'. In Young, M.F.D. (ed.) *Knowledge and Control: New directions for the sociology of education*. London: Collier-Macmillan, 19–46.

# Index

# Index

# Index